## Perfect Persuasion

Richard Storey is an internationally known communication consultant with 30 years' experience. Richard spent the early part of his career in the newspaper advertising industry working as copywriter, trainer and sales manager. He went on to found Sigma Training Services and travels the UK, Europe and the Far East delivering training and development courses, and conference papers. He has written numerous articles for management journals as well as two books: *The Art of Persuasive Communication* (Gower) and *Influencing Pocketbook* (Management Pocketbooks). He recently took a drama degree at Bristol University. Richard's other interests include photography, jazz and cooking. Married with two children, he lives in Bristol.

Should you wish to be coached by Richard, or have him provide a workshop on Perfect Persuasion or speak at a conference, then please email him at: sigmatrainingservices@googlemail.com

Other titles in the *Perfect* series

# Perfect
# Persuasion

**Richard Storey**

BOOKS

Published by Random House Books 2009

10 9 8 7 6 5 4 3 2 1

First published in Great Britain in 2009 by
Random House Books
Random House, 20 Vauxhall Bridge Road,
London SW1V 2SA

www.rbooks.co.uk

This enlarged and updated edition was previously published by Gower
Publishing Limited in 1997 under the title *The Art of Persuasive Communication*.

Addresses for companies within The Random House Group Limited can be
found at: www.randomhouse.co.uk/offices.htm

The Random House Group Limited Reg. No. 954009

A CIP catalogue record for this book
is available from the British Library

ISBN 9781847945594

The Random House Group Limited supports The Forest Stewardship
Council® (FSC®), the leading international forest-certification organisation.
Our books carrying the FSC label are printed on FSC®-certified paper.
FSC is the only forest-certification scheme supported by the leading
environmental organisations, including Greenpeace. Our
paper procurement policy can be found at
www.randomhouse.co.uk/environment

Typeset in Minion by Palimpsest Book Production Limited,
Grangemouth, Stirlingshire

Printed and bound in Great Britain by Clays Ltd, St Ives plc

For my grandson
Arthur

# Contents

# Acknowledgements

People I particularly wish to thank are the many hundreds who have attended my training courses; they remain a constant source of energy, ideas and good persuasion practice.

The relationship between editor and author can be a delicate one, filled with ups and downs, twists and turns. My editor, Sophie Lazar, is a woman of great intellectual discipline. Despite, or because of, her persistence in examining and questioning, making me refine, rewrite and polish sections, I can't thank her enough for her faith in my ability to help readers understand the art and craft of persuasion through this *Perfect* book.

Many thanks to my eagle-eyed friend the journalist Paul Stevens, for vetting the manuscript prior to publication, and for his invaluable, correctly pedantic, and constructive comments.

Thank you, Sue Knight, for your kind permission to use 'Swimming to Japan', reproduced from your exemplary book, *NLP at Work*.

Finally, warm appreciation to Bill Rail: a most inspirational boss. Annoyingly perfectionist, it was he who first alerted me to the notion that the difference between adequate and perfect may often be slight – but in all human endeavour, it is ever the difference that makes the difference.

## Gender point

Words matter, and our language choices have consequences. If we believe that women and men deserve social equality, then we should think seriously about how to reflect that belief in our use of language. To avoid clumsy constructions, throughout this book I have, in most cases, used 'they', 'them' and 'theirs' as substitutes for 'she', 'he', 'hers' or 'his'.

# Introduction

*When the American Management Association surveyed 2,800 executives and asked: 'What is the number one need for success in business today?' the overwhelming response was: 'To persuade others of my value and the value of my ideas.'*

Over many years I have trained thousands of people in the art and craft of persuasion. I am confident no other book demystifies the skills of influential communication in the way that *Perfect Persuasion* does. Every critical aspect of persuasion and influence is explored, deconstructed and explained within the context of recognisable, everyday scenarios. Each chapter offers the inside information you will need to convince others successfully of your value, and the value of your ideas. Tips and techniques on everything from powerful ways to set a compelling vision of where you want to go, through to clinching the deal, are set out in an easy-to-use format that covers the essentials of perfect persuasion. The skills you will learn apply equally to verbal and written communication, face-to-face encounters and contact by telephone. Wherever you are on the ever-continuing cycle of mastery – starting off as a beginner, or experienced and concerned to challenge yourself to new heights of excellence, *Perfect Persuasion* will enable you to maintain your path to more predictable and sustained success. As you move through your journey of life you will find an endless variety of opportunities to use your new skills, over and over. Whenever you feel particularly challenged, it will be a sign that you are learning and growing.

## Who is this book for?

It is for you, when in the future you need to be more effective and need to:

- help others to reach the right conclusion
- persuade others to do something you want them to do
- convince people that your suggestions are of benefit
- make people change their minds, or arrive at some conclusion
- get a decision from someone
- manage a project
- influence senior groups
- convince internal customers
- improve an image or behaviour
- gain acceptance
- negotiate a successful outcome
- gain compliance
- manage expectations
- change perceptions
- manage performance
- change beliefs, perceptions and attitudes

- improve supplier performance
- get ideas past people who have been doing it for years
- write convincing proposals
- change divergence into convergence
- become more successful at networking
- manage relationships
- help others reach the right conclusion
- influence an important outcome
- sell your ideas
- make convincing presentations
- improve your social influence
- influence others on the telephone
- persuade groups or meetings.

*Perfect Persuasion* is for those who want to make their mark in a competitive environment. At work or socially the reader should gain in confidence and see career opportunities develop. Most importantly, perhaps for the first time, you will realise that the power to influence is not exclusively available to those in authority. With hands-on skills and a proactive attitude you too can take charge of your life and career.

The focus of the book is chiefly aimed at influencing one-to-one or within small groups (up to four people) and is designed to take you, step by step, down the path to increased success. You will already know and use some of the techniques and methods it teaches. However, the book is brimful of techniques, tips and hints that are new, or forgotten. When you add these extra tools to your Persuasion Toolkit, persuading others will not only be more rewarding – it will be fun and exciting, too.

## How easy is it to learn persuasion skills?

To become a Perfect Persuader you will need to draw upon a wide selection of possible tactics and styles. A professional mechanic has a toolbox containing every possible tool for the job. In the same way the Persuasion Toolkit contains a variety of powerful and proven tools. This book explores each in turn and suggests ways of learning and practising them until you become the Perfect Persuader.

The secrets of the Perfect Persuader can easily be learned and elegantly used by anyone – even those in a subordinate position. Quick and measurable success can follow and with it the feeling of being ignored by others can become a thing of the past. This book shows you how to persuade and influence others more effectively and – above all – more consistently. Within a short time the desired behaviours will occur naturally and automatically, and unconsciously you will have become perfectly competent. When you next have a particularly important meeting – personal, social or business – where the outcome will rely on your persuasion skills, your Persuasion Toolkit contains all the answers you will need.

Welcome to the age of mastery – enjoy your journey. I am delighted to have become a part of your learning experience.

## How to get the best from your book

The journey towards Perfect Persuasion is never a linear one. So this book is written in a way that allows you to start anywhere. Part one breaks Perfect Persuasion down into its component parts while part two provides the tools and techniques you will need to become a Perfect Persuader. But this is your book, so be as flexible as you wish as you explore its contents. Perhaps you have already mastered the important business of goal-setting but need more help with overcoming objections to your proposals, in which case go straight to part two – Moving on from a 'no'. Perhaps you have difficulty persuading certain personalities. An entire chapter – Who do you think you are? – is devoted to this thorny subject; jump straight to it and find the answers. Many readers will want to read this book from cover to cover, but you can also take it off the shelf and dip into it whenever you need to refresh your memory or reflect on how you can polish your skills even further. Take some time now to assess your present persuasion skills.

## What skills do you need to develop?

If you were to describe yourself as a persuader, what words would you use? Be honest – self-appraisal is the first step towards personal improvement (or be brave and ask someone who knows you well to complete this section for you).

- What are your greatest strengths as a persuader?
- What weaknesses do you have as a persuader?
- Which persuasion situations do you prefer/least prefer?
    - convincing others in business meetings
    - negotiating with professionals
    - selling your ideas to others
    - making convincing presentations
    - persuading people in authority

- writing persuasive reports, letters and emails

- influencing and convincing ditherers

- persuading others over the telephone

- handling tricky personal issues with colleagues or friends

- dealing with conflict

- handling difficult or resistant people

- persuading a social group

- resolving domestic issues equably.

- What would you like people to say about your persuasion skills?

- What sort of persuader do you want to become?

- What evidence will let you know that you have achieved your aims?

  - What will you see?

  - What will you hear?

  - What will you feel?

Now show this self-analysis to a friend or colleague; someone who knows your persuasion style and approach. Do they see you in the same way?

Analyse your feelings about 'persuasion'. How comfortable are you about the process? (For some the word 'persuasion' can be synonymous with 'manipulation'. Individuals who manipulate do so by tricking or setting up other people, usually for personal gain or satisfaction. The benefits are one-sided. If you can satisfy yourself that your successful persuasion offers equal benefit to others and will help maintain a relationship you have with them, you won't want to leave them feeling cheated or short-changed. If we persuade fairly and honourably with a genuine desire to create benefits for others, we can sleep easily with our integrity intact.)

## How to develop your skills

Now you have a clearer idea of which skills you need to concentrate on, you can easily go straight to those parts of the book that deal with the relevant areas. As well as information, hints and tips, you'll also find suggestions for practical ways to hone your skills.

### Exercises and questionnaires

Most chapters offer the opportunity to try things out for yourself. Make the exercises your own by adapting them to suit familiar circumstances, situations or personalities. Get to know yourself better by working through the checklists and questionnaires:

- Persuasion checklist (see page 7)

- Your values and beliefs (see page 25)

- I do it my way (see page 95)

- How do you prefer to communicate? (see page 114)

Check the results with a friend or colleague – do they represent the real you?

### Experimentation

Later in the book you will discover different approaches to persuasion. Experiment with a method that is unusual for you. See where and how it works; adjust it to suit your own style. Use the various styles of persuasion in a pick 'n' mix fashion to handle the different situations in which you will find yourself. Persuading others is an organic, changing process so don't give up easily – constantly dip into your Persuasion Toolkit until you find precisely the right tool for the job.

Learn from your mistakes, actively seek feedback and above all enjoy your path to becoming a Perfect Persuader.

## Role play

Do consider the value of running through your planned persuasion scenario with a colleague or friend. Most people understandably detest the thought of play-acting. We've all been on courses where we have to role-play an untypical scenario in front of a room full of highly critical people – camera, lights, action and so on. However, I am suggesting something altogether different. If you can find someone who knows and understands a bit about your scenario, get together for a while and run through your planned approach. Ask your role player to throw likely objections at you, giving yourself the opportunity to try out a variety of responses. Notice what works and what is less successful. Be aware of your state of mind – how do you feel during certain parts of your role play? Use the feedback you receive to tweak and adjust your final approach.

Role play is especially important if you are planning to persuade a group. Get friends or colleagues to question you or challenge your conclusions and recommendations. I can guarantee that after developing and running a well thought out role play, as they say in the theatre 'on the night', you should experience a wonderfully satisfying feeling of déjà-vu as well as a calm sense of certainty that comes with experience.

# Part one

# Elements of persuasion

# 1 Aim for success

## Setting an objective

*Don't be afraid of the gap between your dreams and reality. If you can dream it, you can do it. Without dreams there is no reality.*

*The more intensely we feel about a goal, the more assuredly the idea, buried deep in our subconscious, will direct us along the path to its fulfilment.*

*Choosing a goal and sticking to it changes everything.*

Most of us have read the inspirational quotes and we all know that goal-setting is important. So why do we do little or nothing about it? Is it because setting objectives is seldom easy? Or because the process itself can seem tedious? Maybe because it's simpler to have high hopes and vague aspirations and not do anything to quantify them or pin them down. To achieve an objective takes concerted effort, commitment and self-discipline, but it's almost always worth the blood, sweat and tears. If you think objective-setting is unnecessary or if you lack the personal discipline needed, you will find it of real practical value to rethink your attitude to objectives and goals.

# Five red hot reasons for setting persuasion objectives

*Great minds have purposes, others have dreams.*

1. All Perfect Persuaders, leaders, business executives, entrepreneurs, scientists, sportspeople, artists, designers and inventors share a common characteristic: they believe in goal-setting.

2. People with clear goals succeed because they know where they're going.

3. Objective-setting is arguably the single most important aspect of the persuasion process.

4. Setting clearly defined objectives and writing them down actually works.

5. People who commit to written goals for themselves are demonstrably more successful as a result.

# How we programme our brain to achieve unconscious objectives

> *You are moulding your tomorrow based on what you do today . . . Find out what it is you want, and go after it as if your life depends on it. Why? Because it does.*
> Les Brown, author and motivational speaker, 1945–

You may or may not be consciously aware that you already set objectives for yourself. As you live your days, weeks and years you are constantly moving towards objective achievement. Take a simple procedure – getting up in the morning to go to work. There are things you do automatically. You brush your teeth, shower, dress, eat breakfast, leave the house. There may be other things that you could do: repaint the front door, read a novel, clean the bathroom, telephone your aunt in Australia. But you don't. These tasks may be on your 'to do list' but you put them to one side because you know unconsciously that they would prevent you from reaching your objective of getting to work. You have objectives all the time, if only to do absolutely nothing but relax. With no *conscious* objectives you would be aimless and achieve very little.

Within larger objectives, such as getting to work, are smaller ones. For instance, when you dress you may wish to look smart, so you check your clothing is clean – almost without realising it. This is because you've set your objective and find yourself automatically moving towards it without considering each small step along the way. Our conscious minds can handle up to nine separate pieces of information at any one time. As we get out of bed, we're already thinking about our bathroom routine, mentally running through our first meeting at the same time as we listen to the radio and peer out of the window to examine today's weather. Yet during these complex thought processes we get our bodies to perform micro muscle movements and incredible mechanical feats without consciously asking it to. If we had to think about several hundred things at once, our conscious minds simply couldn't cope. So we select what to pay attention to. We sort what to do, what to ignore and to what we should give our time and energy. Our criteria for whether actions or thoughts are useful to us are generated by knowing where we want to go. Once programmed our brains enable us to achieve our unconscious objectives without much thought or effort.

# Why it is important to understand how you are persuaded

A useful way to begin to get to grips with this business of setting specific objectives is to analyse what it is that convinces you.

Think back to a time when another person successfully persuaded you. Recall the steps or elements of their influence. What did they do or say that convinced you? What were the key words and phrases that hit the right button? Where did the conversation take place? What was their manner like? What was your own frame of mind, or mood? If you used the same approach with others, could you be sure that it would be as effective? Chances are that you would need to make modifications to your approach, changes that would take into account:

- your frame of mind

- the other person's mood

- their age

- their gender

- their cultural background

- their relationship to you

- their understanding or experience of the subject

- the time of day, week or year

- the location of the meeting

- their willingness or desire to listen

- their interpretative skills

- their willingness to be influenced by you

- the way in which they like to make decisions.

## Persuasion checklist

Before setting your objectives, it is important to ask yourself a few questions about your forthcoming meeting or presentation. This checklist, while not exhaustive, will help you to design your own list. Use it as a template. After a while, you will begin to answer most of the questions instinctively, but until you are an experienced persuader, use your checklist as an aide-memoire.

- Person, people, meeting participants, group or audience to be influenced.
- Your objectives? What do you want to happen as a result of your successful influence?
- Their objectives – what do they want to happen?
- What gap if any exists between your objectives and their objectives?

Analysis of the other person/people involved:

A. Their knowledge of the subject:
❑ High level  ❑ General  ❑ Limited
❑ None  ❑ Unknown

B. Their likely opinions about you/your motives/the subject/your organisation:
❑ Very favourable  ❑ Favourable  ❑ Neutral
❑ Slightly hostile  ❑ Very hostile  ❑ Unknown

C. Their reasons or motives for attending

D. Advantages and disadvantages of your objectives to them as individuals, or as a group

E. General analysis (work related):

What are their occupational relationships to you, your department or organisation?

- ❑ Existing customer
- ❑ New customer
- ❑ Top management
- ❑ Middle management
- ❑ People you manage
- ❑ Other management
- ❑ Other colleagues
- ❑ The public
- ❑ Outside agencies

Their familiarity with your company's business activities?

- ❑ Very familiar
- ❑ Moderately familiar
- ❑ Unfamiliar

Their understanding of your technical vocabulary?

- ❑ Technical
- ❑ Non technical
- ❑ Generally high
- ❑ Low
- ❑ Unknown

Open-mindedness – willingness to accept new ideas?

- ❑ Eager
- ❑ Open
- ❑ Neutral
- ❑ Slightly resistant
- ❑ Strongly resistant
- ❑ Unknown

Information most likely to gain their attention and influence this audience?

- ❑ Highly technical information
- ❑ Statistical comparisons
- ❑ Pictures
- ❑ Cost figures
- ❑ Metaphor
- ❑ Demonstrations
- ❑ Lecture style
- ❑ Questions
- ❑ Dialogue
- ❑ Anecdotal evidence
- ❑ Unknown

Techniques/information likely to provoke negative attitudes/responses?

• Summarise, in a few sentences/phrases, the most important information gained from the preceding sections.

## Clarifying your conscious objectives

Before you commence your plan to persuade, think clearly about your objectives. What do you want to happen as a result of influencing this person or group? Here are some questions you may want to ask yourself even before you start to formulate and write down your fully formed objective statement. Use the checklist above and be sure that you have the answers to the following questions:

• Why do I want to convince this person?

• What will I gain when I succeed in doing so?

• What are their objectives?

• What will they gain from my influence?

• Are there any ethical or moral concerns I need to consider?

• Will my success in persuading be of mutual benefit?

• When I have succeeded, will my integrity remain intact?

• Will any other people be adversely affected by the outcome?

• Will my success in any way alter future attempts to persuade this person?

## A kind of magic – how Perfect Persuaders set conscious objectives

Suppose you have an important meeting with a friend or a colleague, one where you will be required to state your case and convince them. You have time to work out your strategy, to consider how you will handle objections to your proposal and so on. You also have time to set personal objectives. At the beginning of this chapter we acknowledged that we often talk about the importance of objective-setting; we pay lip service to it but rarely do more than say something like:

1. 'I really want to win them over.'
2. 'I know I am right and I am going to try and sell them the idea.'
3. 'I don't want this to go on any longer and I am going to convince them to stop doing it.'
4. 'I hope to persuade them that they are making the wrong decision.'

These are not fully formed objective statements – they are merely hopes, aspirations, wish lists. 'Nothing wrong with that,' some might say. 'At least I have *got* an idea of what I want to achieve.' There is no harm in having a rough idea of what you want, or to set out to achieve something specific, attainable and lasting. But there is a world of difference between the two approaches.

Stop for a moment and analyse the four 'objectives' listed above.

1. *'I really want to win them over.'*
   Full marks for determination. But determination alone will not necessarily mean that your objectives 'to win them over' are met.

2. *'I know I am right and I am going to try and sell them the idea.'*
   The very inclusion of the verb 'to try' acknowledges the possibility of failure.

3. *'I don't want this to go on any longer and I am going to do my best to convince them to stop doing it.'*
   This is a negative objective. You are attempting to convince people *not* to do something.

4. *'I hope to persuade them that they are making the wrong decision.'*
   The aspiration 'I hope' is rather like 'to try' and incorporates the likelihood of only partial success or even downright failure.

## Step one – think positively

Make certain that your objective is stated in the *positive;* think of what you *want* rather than what you don't want.

> **Example:** 'I don't want this to go on any longer.'
> **Q.** 'What would you prefer to happen?'
> **A.** 'I want things to go right in future.'

'I don't want this to go on any longer' gives you nothing specific to go towards.

## Step two – put yourself in charge

Do you own the outcome or is it another person's? (For example, a friend tells you: 'I think you should lose weight.' That is *their* outcome, not yours.) Think of the part you will play in achieving the outcome. Make certain that the possibility of achievement is within your control, not someone else's.

> **Q.** 'What will I be doing to achieve my objective?' Or, 'What is my part in this?'
>
> **A.** 'I want to make certain I am the one who sets the agenda for the meeting.'

Rather than 'I will go along with the agenda and hope there will be a moment when I can get my point across', which is out of your complete control.

Be aware that you will come upon barriers to your success. How will you overcome these? (Barriers also represent a test of your resolve. As the late Professor Randy Pausch said: 'Brick walls are there for a reason. They let us prove how badly we want things.')

## Step three – be specific

State your objective in manageable proportions that also make it seem real: something definite to go for, which begins to suggest genuine actions towards getting to the outcome.

> **Q.** 'Who will I meet? What will I say? When will I talk to them? How will I approach it? Which method will I choose? Where will this take place?'
>
> **A.** 'I will meet the subcommittee at their next meeting and make a presentation to them at the end of the meeting. I will raise some questions and ask them what they want. Finally, I will ask for a decision and an action plan.'

Rather than 'I want our club to be more successful' – a statement that is too vague.

## Step four – use evidence

Obtain evidence criteria. This is the sensory information which lets you know when you've got what you want. This will make your objective far more real and compelling. Use all your senses:

* sight – the evidence you will see

* sound – the evidence you will hear

* feeling (1) – the evidence you sense emotionally

* feeling (2) – the evidence you will touch

* smell – the evidence you will smell

* taste – the evidence you will taste.

I was recently helping a friend to set some influencing objectives. She wanted to persuade her husband to join her on a much-needed holiday in Greece. When it came to deciding what evidence would prove to Gill that she had achieved her objective, I asked her:

> **Q.** 'What will you see, hear and feel both inside and outside that will let you know you have achieved your objective?'
>
> **A.** 'I will *see* the cloudless blue sky above me and *hear* the soft sound of waves; Greek music is wafting through the olive grove and I hear the clink of ice in the glass in my hand. I will *feel* the sun on my body and the cold glass in my hand. I will *smell* sun oil and *taste* the ouzo in the glass.'

Her answer was more substantial and robust than 'I'll just know when I am successful', which usually means just the opposite. You probably have no idea of your own 'buying signals' yet.

(Later that summer Gill called me: 'That outcome-setting

exercise you did with me was amazing. As soon as I got to the island and lay on the beach it all came flooding back to me. The sights and sounds, the smells and tastes – just as we discussed. It made the hairs on the back of my neck stand up. Magic!')

## Step five – check the integrity

Check that you will get only the consequences you really want. Will you be entirely happy with the outcome? Will your success adversely affect anyone else? Notice any doubts that start 'Yes, but . . .'

> **Q.** 'Does any part of me object in any way to achieving my objective?' Or, 'If I could achieve my objective right now, would I take it without reservation?'

If the answer were to be a doubtful 'Yes, but . . .'; or 'Well, I'm not sure'; 'As long as it didn't affect such and such . . .' and so on, there are obviously other considerations or conditions which must be woven into the objective. These will enable it to become an acceptable one to achieve with purely positive consequences. The 'acceptability' area is where most problems occur; people think they should attempt to achieve an objective, but deep down are worried about some spin-off consequences. If you are not fully committed at this stage, you are unlikely to achieve your objective.

## In short

The five-step path described above can be summarised as follows:

1. Write down your objective statement. Check to make sure it is stated positively.

2. Make sure you have full control over the outcome.

3. Be specific about the ways you will go about achieving your objective.

4. Ask yourself: what evidence will I see, hear, feel, smell or taste which will confirm that I have achieved my objective?

5. Check the integrity and acceptability of your objective.

## The power of creative visualisation

In his book *Psychocybernetics*, Dr Maxwell Maltz clarified a profound truth: the subconscious mind does not know the difference between a real and an imagined event. In other words, it is perfectly possible to programme our brains towards achieving a set goal. The golfer Tiger Woods visualises the ball going into the hole then tracks the shot backwards, towards where he is positioned in order to understand what he has to do to get the ball in the hole.

If all this sounds like so much psychobabble, try this little experiment: close your eyes and relax. Imagine you are holding a fat, ripe lemon. Weigh it in your hand, feel its coolness, savour the strong citrus smell given off from the waxy skin. Now, imagine you are cutting into it with a sharp knife. Peel away the skin and notice the juice already seeping out from the glistening segments. Feel your mouth salivating as you imagine biting into a piece, the juices squirting out on to your tongue. Your creative imagination alone has induced a physical response; your mouth starts to produce saliva.

Maxwell Maltz said that one of the great truths in the world of humans is that you become what you think about all day long. If you see yourself bright, cheerful and successful, it will work wonders in your life. If you see yourself as a failure and unsuccessful, you have created a blueprint for your subconscious mind to follow. Not only does your subconscious mind not know the difference between a real and an imagined event, it does not choose between what's good for you or what's bad for you. It just follows the 'orders' you 'give it' – just like a computer follows the programming that goes in. If you put garbage in, you get garbage out. It's as true for our minds as it is for our computers.

## Brace yourself for success

You have now set yourself up for success. Your mind and body think your objectives have already been achieved. You will start to act and talk differently, more positively. Of course some readers may still think that this mind-over-matter stuff is complete nonsense – until they do it for themselves and discover that it really does work. Once you make this work for yourself, you will never look back and creative visualisation will become an everyday part of your continuing success.

The art of visualising a future outcome is arguably the single most powerful self-development tool you can use when influencing others or aiming for any other objective. However, do not fall into the trap of limiting your success by setting yourself rigid process elements. These might include phrases such as 'By the end of the meeting I will have convinced . . . '; or 'The committee members will resolve . . . ' You may run the risk of painting yourself into a corner and may consider that you have 'failed' before you have had the opportunity of exploring all the options available to you.

# Rehearsal: the best investment you'll make

*Practice is the best of all instructors*
Publilius Syrus, writer, 1st century BC

Part of the planning process should include some sort of rehearsal or run-through of the scenario. This can take one of three forms:

1. Simply going over your approach in your head.

2. Talking it through with a friend or colleague.

3. A full-blown role play preferably recorded for later evaluation.

Most people detest role play and this is understandable. But its value cannot be stressed too highly. A while back a colleague and I had to conduct a negotiation with two other people. As we drove to the meeting we started to run through the forthcoming dialogue. We asked ourselves questions: 'What do we really want to get from the negotiation? What is the most we could achieve? What is the least we would be prepared to accept? What are we likely to get? Suppose they say such and such – how will we respond? If we responded in that way, would they agree with what we said? If not, what could we suggest as an alternative? What variables can we trade, what is their value?' And so on.

Although it was intended that I would conduct the negotiation, in the end my colleague felt so confident after the brief run-through that they carried it out. With a few minor exceptions we came away with exactly what we wanted – plus one or two surprising extras.

Role play is rather like a sparring match. The boxer preparing for the big fight, will use a sparring partner. It is not the intention of either man to knock one another out or to inflict serious damage. Rather, the value of the sparring match is that it allows the champion-to-be to try things out, to see how he will react on the night.

If you can, use either video or audio recordings to provide the basis of self-analysis. It can be quite a shock seeing or hearing yourself for the first time on tape. But once this reaction is over, the value which you can derive from seeing or hearing yourself is very powerful and useful. You will notice the times when you felt and acted most confidently. You will spot the weaknesses in your approach, style or argument. You will make changes and improve your strategy. You will be more confident of your abilities and will look forward to a successful dialogue or meeting.

# 2  The important things in life
## What motivates people

Imagine the scene. You are walking down the street when a passer-by stops you. 'Can I have a word? Good. I have the most incredible bargain to offer you. It's a Jaguar sports coupé in silver, only eighteen months old with less than 30,000 kilometres on the clock. It cost more than £50,000, but to you I can let it go for £25,000 – that's half price. How about it? What do you think?'

Well, what would you think? You may produce a cheque book and snap up what is evidently a real bargain. You may disbelieve the person – who are they? Do they really own the car? You may have suspicions about the car – is it roadworthy? Has it been stolen, or been in a crash? And the price. Did it really cost £50,000 eighteen months ago? Is it worth less than £25,000 now?

Worse still – you may not be motivated to buy such a car. Suppose you can't drive? Your family is too large for a coupé. You can't stand the colour. You've never liked Jaguar cars. You are happy with your present vehicle. You can't afford £25,000. Perhaps you normally pay even more than that for a car.

Unless you have power over people it is difficult to influence anybody who does not have the motivation to say 'yes'. Advertising people will tell you that in order to bring about change there are only three motivators:

1. need

2. greed

3. fear.

This assumption may be accurate, but it is also an oversimplification. Many of our decisions are motivated by a *combination* of these motivators. Take, as an example, life assurance. The primary motivator is fear – but a with-profits policy allows us to borrow money against future profits, an additional factor that may appeal to additional needs (or greed).

Convincing people they have a need is quite easy and straightforward. But convincing them to change as a result of this knowledge is difficult. Why? Because people resist change. They may accept that needs exist, but other things get in the way:

- lack of funds

- lack of time

- loyalty to current system/idea/person/product/supplier/contract

- sheer complacency

- fear of making the wrong decision.

Thus, although recognition of need is very powerful, change may only be brought about when it is accompanied by greed or fear (or both). I have a need to change my car. It is old, has a high mileage and is becoming increasingly unreliable. But I don't have the money. I could be persuaded to borrow the money through a finance scheme but normally pay cash. What might change my mind? Perhaps there is another car that interests me but there is only one left in the showroom (fear); the deal which is being offered expires on Saturday (greed); the new car is a 'special edition' and appeals to my vanity (additional and unspoken need).

## What is motivation?

Motivation is what makes us act or behave in the way we do. If we want to influence others to change we ask: 'How can I motivate them? What are their needs?'

There are two famous classifications of needs, one formulated by Abraham Maslow, the other by Frederick Herzberg. Maslow suggests that humans have a simple hierarchy of needs; one need has to be satisfied before the next one emerges.

Herzberg's research suggested that motivators at work fell into two categories. The first factors spring from the work itself and include: job satisfaction, recognition, a sense of achievement, good communication, belonging and social acceptance, which are real motivators. They appear to be continuous and genuinely spur us on to even better performance and effort.

The second group of needs (Herzberg's so-called 'hygiene factors' – things extrinsically provided by the employer) appear to be motivators but in fact are not and can even be 'demotivators'. These hygiene factors include: the work environment, pay, holidays, training – and are all designed to *prevent* job dissatisfaction. For example, a pay rise is very satisfying and a good short-term motivator. But is only short term. From the moment we bank our new salary the increase in our pay progressively decreases in value, both in real terms and eventually in how pleased we feel about it.

Motivation is a forward-looking process, starting with those needs and wants that exist in us all.

- Needs create action.

- Action achieves goals.

- Achieving a goal satisfies a need.

This process closely follows the path we tread when influencing:

1. Identify the other person's needs and suggest a solution.

2. Their consequent action achieves the solution as well as ours.

3. This achievement satisfies both their needs and ours.

## How to identify motivations and needs

Most people make the mistake of assuming that our personal motivations are universal: 'What motivates me must motivate the other person.' Nothing could be further from the truth. You may strike lucky – yes, it turns out that they are motivated by the same things that you are. But in fact, values, beliefs, needs and wants are far more complex than we tend to think.

We are all driven by those things we regard to be important in our lives. These might include a house of our own, a healthy bank balance, a loving relationship, praise and appreciation from those we look up to, and so on. Some people are driven by what might be regarded as negative motivations: greed for more, envy of others, fear of failure. Although negative, these drives are every bit as powerful as positive motivators.

## Top 20 basic human motivations

- Recognition
- Security
- Convenience
- Saving
- Profit
- Health
- Appetite
- Education
- Comfort
- Enjoyment
- Self-approval
- Culture
- Fashion
- Religion
- Love/affection
- Compassion
- Fear*
- Greed*
- Vanity*
- Sex*

* These motivations can also be weaknesses. It is questionable to exploit these in others for the sake of influencing change – unless of course you can convince yourself that the change brought about is seen to have a positive outcome or that these needs are in themselves positive.

To influence others it is vitally important to understand as much as we can about their motivations. What do they see as important considerations? What might put them off? Broadly speaking, motivators can be subdivided into:

- values

- beliefs

- needs

- wants.

Some people are better than others at observing behaviours and identifying what motivates them. Others base their judgements on a 'gut feeling' which is often unreliable. There are three simple ways to understand what motivates others:

1. Observe for ourselves, conclude and verify our conclusions.

2. Ask the other person what motivates them (not as daft as it sounds). Observe what they tell you and verify its truth.

3. Ask someone else – a person who knows the individual concerned and has sufficient relevant experience on which to base reliable judgement. Once again – observe and verify.

## Don't mess with the other person's values

Values are about who you want to be. They vary so much from person to person that there can be no hard and fast 'rules' to follow. However, they might include some of the following: honesty, faithfulness, integrity, achievement, love, independence, self-esteem, self-belief, self-confidence, success. These can be ranked in some arbitrary order. For example, a person may rate integrity and honesty higher than success. Or self-confidence over achievement.

In influencing there are three main points to bear in mind:

1. Knowing the other person's values may be vitally important when the time comes to work out your strategy. If they regard integrity highly and you make proposals that compromise that value, you will fail.

2. Values tend to persist. They are formed over time. Perhaps they spring from the other person's upbringing. Maybe they form part of a religious or philosophical teaching. Possibly the values derive from an especially influential relationship.

3. Values can be so rooted in a person's psyche that it will almost certainly be counterproductive to try to shift them.

> *In matters of principle, stand firm like a rock.*
> *In matters of opinion, flow like a river.*
> Thomas Jefferson, US President, 1743–1826

## How we are controlled by our beliefs and opinions

Beliefs and opinions are commonly confused with values. The two are very different. While a value is usually deeply rooted and difficult to remove, beliefs can ebb and flow throughout a person's life. They are in a constant state of flux. Set firm today, challenged tomorrow. Learned at school, changed within months of leaving. Told by a trusted friend, later dismissed as nonsense. You will remember when you used to believe in Father Christmas or the Tooth Fairy or giants. Here are some examples of typical universal beliefs:

- My country/religion/team is the best.

- All salespeople are out to con the customer.

- Politicians are not to be believed.

- Certain makes of car/dishwasher/watch are more reliable than others.

## Your values and beliefs

In order to understand how other people's values and beliefs may affect the way in which they are influenced, take a few minutes now to examine your own. Notice how they affect the ways in which you make decisions.

1. List the five values which you regard as most important. At the same time remember how you came to hold these values. Where did the influence come from? Your parents? School? Religion? Relations? Friends? Neighbours? Society? Your culture?

2. Now note three beliefs which you no longer regard as true. At the same time, note what or who influenced your change of mind.

Understanding your values and beliefs, and why you would be prepared to have them changed, puts you in a far better position to think about how you approach persuading or influencing others.

# Needs need satisfying

Much has been written about needs and what motivates human beings. For the purposes of persuasion it can be argued that there is little sense in wasting time distinguishing between a *need* and a *want*. Whether a person insists that they have a real need that remains unsatisfied, or that they simply want something, is academic. All we have to do is fulfil the requirement. Here are some standard needs:

- to save money

- to avoid spending money

- to save time

- to save effort

- to assert oneself

- to be secure

- to be independent

- to act

- to make more money

- to gain a discount

- to be seen to make the 'right' decision

- to meet a specification

- to be superior

- to defend/preserve

- to discover

- to conquer.

And some wants:

- to be first
- to win a negotiation
- to have the cheapest solution
- to be different

- to be liked

- to possess or collect

- to imitate and identify

- to have the best

- to get something for nothing

- to have the most expensive solution

- to be envied

- to be comfortable

- to feel pleased and happy

- to do nothing.

You may have noticed that while the needs are tangible and measurable, the wants tend to be subjective. In other words, if a person thinks they have the best or cheapest solution, then they do. But don't dismiss wants simply because they are difficult to measure. They can be more powerful than the more tangible and objective needs.

## What's in it for the other person?

To get the best from this exercise it is helpful if you have a real example or case study to work with. If not, create a hypothetical example.

1. Think of a future situation where you want to persuade a person or people. Decide on your objective and write it down.

2. Put yourself in the other person's shoes. Imagine you are the one who will be making the decision to say 'yes' or 'no' to the proposition.

3. What are the most important or significant needs which you want fulfilling?

4. Beyond the needs, is there anything that you or others would want? Be imaginative, try to avoid being influenced by your own set of criteria. This is an exercise in creative speculation. Speculate, creatively!

## Power words

Throughout your future influencing dialogue with others you will, of course, be using words. Whether face-to-face at a meeting or presentation, one-to-one, over the telephone or in writing, the words you choose to use can have enormous bearing on your success.

Understand the needs of others and you will understand the power words that can transform a mundane suggestion into an irresistible invitation. Take a few tips from the experts in extracting a positive response – direct mail and mail order companies. They live or die by their abilities to influence our buying decisions. All of us are bombarded by junk mail, so what is it that separates the letters from successful mail order companies (such as Reader's Digest) from those that we throw away without even opening?

Top presenters, speakers, teachers and trainers use the words *you*, *we* and *I* extensively. They include their audience at all times in what they are saying or doing. For instance, 'You and I both know that this makes sense, don't we?' enrols the audience into the assumption that what is being said *does* make sense.

A number of words in the English language have been identified as being more powerful than others. They are words that are more likely to stimulate a response in us when we hear or read them. They are words that have a magnetic attraction for all of us.

Yale University made a study of 'power words' and concluded that the most effective words were those that affect us most directly. Some examples include: You/yours, easy, love, now, trouble-free, positive, discover, win/winning, power, secret/secrets, how to, save, guarantee, free, health, success, will, greatest, proven, results, new, safe, most, best, pleased, when, tested, unique, excellence, announcing, like you, must.

With your new list of power words you now have proven success tips that are easy to use. You will find yourself using these winning words in future influencing situations with positive results.

*You* and *yours* are the most powerful words you can use when influencing others. This is because they appeal directly and unequivocally to the individual or group. There is no doubt about it – your proposal or idea is aimed at *them*. (The introduction to this book includes the words you/your/yourself around a hundred times.)

*The entire sales force of Perky Cat Food Company was gathered for the annual sales convention. Two thousand salespeople were listening intently to the marketing director who was waving his arms about on the podium, giving a most enthusiastic perform-ance. Like an old-world revivalist he was getting his sales force really hyped up.*

'*Who's got the greatest cat food in the world?*'
'*We have!*'

'And who's got the best advertising campaign?'

'We have!!'

'Who has the most attractive packaging?'

'We have!!!'

'Who has the best distribution network?'

'WE HAVE!'

'OK. So why aren't we selling more of our product?'

One bold salesperson at the back shouted: 'Because cats don't like it.'

# 3 What exactly do you mean?
## Asking the right questions

We all filter reality and make our own map of the world as we see it. But maps are selective and leave out information as well as providing it. In order to persuade someone, it is important to get inside their map of reality, to see and understand the territory as they see and understand it.

Let's suppose that you want to convince a friend to join you for a short holiday. Frankly, you need a break. Work has been demanding lately and you know that a few days away will do you the world of good. You have seen an advertisement for a small country hotel. It is not expensive and has a reputation for French food. It is far enough away to provide variety but not too far to travel to. You get a brochure and decide to tell your friend all about your exciting idea.

You are very surprised when they turn down your proposal. You cannot understand why they do not see the benefits. You feel rejected and dejected. But had you taken the trouble to check a few points before making your proposal, perhaps your ideas would have met with more success. The right words can strike notes on the keyboard of the imagination.

# Planning to persuade – an exercise in empathy

Using the example above (the proposed weekend break with a friend) or an example of your own, imagine that you are the person to be influenced. Sit back, shut your eyes and put yourself in their shoes.

Now, ask yourself what criteria would have to be met if you were to agree to a weekend break with a friend. Think of headings under which you could develop a simple checklist. Here are some to start with – you add to the list:

- hotel

- location

- things to do

- food I like.

This analysis will confirm either that you are on the right lines and will be able to convince your friend, or that you may have to make some changes to your proposal.

Now put yourself in the shoes of the person who is to be persuaded. Questions which you may want to ask yourself could include: Do you need a holiday right now? Do you like short holiday breaks? What do you think of country hotels? Which do you prefer – small or large hotels? What can you afford? Which parts of the country appeal to you? Would you prefer to holiday abroad? Do you have any special dietary requirements?

You must establish as early as you can whether the other person will feel that they need what you are proposing. Planning and preparation will answer many of your questions – but not all. Be warned – a lot of time spent attempting to influence can be wasted by failing to ask yourself quite basic questions from the start. This is because we do not see the world entirely from the same point of view.

> *The Universe is not an idea of mine;*
> *My idea of the universe is an idea of mine.*
> *Night doesn't fall before my eyes;*
> *My idea of night falls before my eyes.*
> Fernando Pessoa, Portuguese poet and writer,
> 1888–1935

## Will I be wasting my time?

Your intentions may be sound, your proposition watertight – but can the other person say 'yes'? Do they have the resources, the time, the will? Professional persuaders set great store by what is called 'pre-call planning'. It can be time well spent and a worthwhile investment. Naturally, it is impossible to provide a comprehensive list of dos and don'ts which will apply to all circumstances. However, the following checklist should cover most situations.

- Can this person make the decision to buy my proposal?

- Do I know or can I guess their needs?

- Are there any technical specifications that must be met?

- Are there any other people whose influence may carry weight?

- Is there an intended time scale – yours or theirs?

- Is there a budget? How realistic is it?

- How will any costs be met?

- How do they typically make decisions?

- Does the thinking behind your proposition make sense?

## Asking questions

Most influencers use questions to discover useful information and to lead the other person towards a decision. This rather basic approach is limiting and can often fail. Here is an example:

Shop assistant: May I help you?
Customer: No thank you. I'm just looking.

When will they ever learn? Over and over, day after day – same question, same response. Quite often a statement rather than a question will do the trick.

Shop assistant: Good afternoon. If you have any questions, just let me know. Please feel free to look around.
Customer: Well, I was wondering if you have that colour in a size 42?

*Or*

Shop assistant: Good morning – those shirts you're looking at are new in this week. What size are you looking for?
Customer: Have you got a 42?

## Different types of question

There is a wide variety of questions from which you can choose, depending on your desired outcome and response. Here are some examples:

**1. Open questions.** Any question starting with Who, What, How, Why, Where or When is likely to avoid a 'yes' or 'no' answer. These are useful for probing and digging for deeper needs.
**Examples:** 'When does this kind of problem arise?'; 'How important to you is a solution?'

**2. Closed questions** are used when you require a yes/no response, an agreement or a short answer. As these questions will obtain less information you may risk proceeding with less understanding of the other's needs. They are best employed when you want to cut to the chase and obtain agreement.
**Examples:** 'Shall we go ahead?'; 'Are you happy with that idea?'

**3. Reflective questions** spring from the content of previous answers. They are psychologically powerful because they 'reflect' something the other person has said or feels and provide certain proof of your empathy and listening skills.
**Example:** 'Going back to your earlier point about performance, how important is that to you?'

**4. Multiple questions** are several questions masquerading as a single question. They can provide a useful primer question to initiate dialogue but are potentially confusing. Also, they offer the other person the option of choosing which part of your multiple question to answer. Use with care and deliberation.

**Example:** 'What did you like about the job . . . was it the people, the location, the type of business or your manager . . . ?

**5. Leading questions**. Any question which *leads* the other person towards a response you wish or expect them to make is a leading question. This is a form of questioning which many people resist. Use occasionally.
**Example:** 'You're not happy about that, are you?'

**6. Assumptive questions.** Such questions contain an assumption – therefore to disagree, the other person has to remove your assumption. Often, people will go along with an assumption if it is prefaced with words such as: 'obviously', 'clearly', 'I'm sure you'll agree'.
**Example:** 'So you obviously support Sophie's point of view?'

**7. Add-on questions** are statements that have an additional phrase on the end. Similar to the assumptive, they are more subtle.
**Example:** 'That's often the case, *isn't it*?'
Other add-on questions include: 'Aren't they?' 'Don't you?' 'Couldn't it?' 'Isn't that right?' 'Shouldn't we?' 'Don't you agree?'

**8. Alternative choice questions**. These are the salesperson's best friend: the so-called 'tea or coffee close'. This technique forces the other person to make a choice from what is offered. More powerful than asking: 'Do you like the red one?'
**Examples:** 'Which of these two packaging designs do you prefer – the red or the green one?'

**9. Background questions** give you basic information from which you can draw conclusions.
**Example:** 'What was it that led Mike to make that decision?'

**10. Problem questions** focus on deeper aspects of the other person's situation or problem. Imagine peeling an onion. Layer after layer of flesh comes away before you reach the core.

**Examples:** 'What kind of problems did that produce?' (Note the use of an open, assumptive question. If you asked, 'Did that produce any problems?' this could allow the other person to say 'no'.) 'So how effective was your solution?' 'If there had been a different solution, what would that have been?'

**11. Effect questions** define what could happen as a result of the prevailing situation or problem.

**Example:** 'So what will be the outcome if nothing is done about that?'

**12. Need questions** allow the person to state their requirements in their terms; this will help reinforce their commitment to your proposed solutions or suggestions.

**Example:** 'If you had that, how useful would it be to you in the future?'

## Different perspectives

Each of us has our own language, based on personal experience. These experiences colour the way we see the world. To be able fully to understand other people, we need also to be able to understand their ways of thinking. Each person's understanding of what goes on around them is their 'reality'. Curiously, theirs may not be the same 'reality' that we ourselves understand. There is a well-known anecdote concerning Sir Walter Raleigh which illustrates this point. While imprisoned in the Tower of London and writing his *Historie of the World*, a disturbance took place beneath his window. He asked several people what had happened but received numerous, conflicting accounts. Raleigh remarked that he was naïve to rely on stories of historical events for his book, when it was impossible to arrive at the truth of what had just taken place in the courtyard below. We do see the world through different eyes. Have you ever been on a walk with a friend and noticed or heard or smelt different things? This is quite common. Ask two people to describe the person they witnessed robbing a bank and you could be looking for two robbers – the descriptions may be that different.

Reality – whatever that means – can only be described in words. Reality is what other people believe it to be. When we describe our version of reality we create our description from sensory-based language – what we saw, heard, touched, felt emotionally, smelt or tasted. That is it. We have no more ways of talking about our understanding. This is why communication can go so badly wrong.

All nouns can be divided into two categories:

• specific, definite, concrete

• vague, abstract, nominalisations.

Some examples of each 'type':

| SPECIFIC | VAGUE |
| --- | --- |
| book | trust |
| silk | motivation |
| path | quality |
| car | loyalty |
| nails | effectiveness |
| manager | worry |
| field | productivity |
| wall | security |

My dictionary defines 'friend' as 'A person for whom one feels affection; whom one knows intimately; companion; helper; colleague; associate; acquaintance.' The definition offers seven possible interpretations. Which friend, specifically? Who, exactly, do you mean? Precisely how friendly? What do you mean, specifically? Friendly under what circumstances?

If three people are discussing 'productivity' each could be using the word from a different perspective (perhaps associated with past experience or future expectations). 'Productivity – the rate at which something is produced,' declares my dictionary. Produced by what, specifically? People? Machines? Department? Company? Productivity of what?

## PowerQuestions

If you want to discover what a person really means in their communication and how consequent thought processes might affect behaviour you only need to learn one set of questions, which I call PowerQuestions. To take someone where you want to go, you have to know where they are at the moment. To influence their ideas, you have to know what those ideas are. These PowerQuestions will become the most powerful and important you will ever learn. They can cut through verbal fog like a scalpel.

Before we look at the PowerQuestions themselves, you will need to recognise the moment in a conversation when you will want to use one of these questions. Just as there are a number of questions to ask, there are also some signals which will enable you to use the appropriate PowerQuestion:

- when a statement made by another person has information missing from it

- when statements contain apparent rules, limitations or gener-
  alisations

- when statements suggest a distorted view of reality.

## How to make PowerQuestions work for you

Most Perfect Persuaders know about and use PowerQuestions. They recognise their value when used in conversations where things seem to have ground to a halt. Here are some examples of ways in which you might detect the moment and know which PowerQuestion will come to your rescue. The examples given are brief, to help you learn the technique. In real life, however, it is often useful to soften the question. For example: 'Oh, that's interesting . . .'; 'I know what you mean . . .'; 'That's a good point you've raised . . .'; 'Can I just ask . . .'; or simply repeat the statement back to them. The technique works best when there is excellent rapport – where each person wants to achieve the same outcome.

## Find the missing information

Some people delete words on purpose; they want to avoid clarity or are reluctant to go deeper into issues. Sometimes a word is acci-dentally missed out altogether, so that the meaning is incomplete or ambiguous. To make sense of the statement we need to recover the missing word.

Every parent will recognise this dialogue which I had with my daughter (at the time 16 years old):

Me: Where are you going?
Lottie: Out to meet some friends.
Me: Which friends?

Lottie: Don't know yet, depends on who turns up.
Me: Where are you meeting them?
Lottie: In a pub.
Me: Which pub?
Lottie: One in town.
Me: When will you be home?
Lottie: Late.
Me: How late is 'late'?
Lottie: After midnight.
Me (desperate by now): How long after midnight? When should I begin to worry about you?

Deliberate evasion is easy. Just leave out the facts, the specifics, the adjectives and adverbs. It is not always a matter of deliberate deception through evasion. Perhaps the other person knows their subject matter so thoroughly that they mistakenly believe they have included certain pieces of important information, or that you have that information already.

Here are some examples of statements that contain 'missing' or 'deleted' information and the PowerQuestion which should solve the riddle.

## Nouns which mean nothing to you

These PowerQuestions elicit specific information about the noun used.

'I am going to the *shop*.'
'*Which shop, specifically?*'

'*Profits* are looking good this year.'
'*Which profits, exactly?*'

'I want a *new job.*'
'*Precisely what kind of new job?*'

'*They* don't listen to me.'
'*Who exactly doesn't listen to you?*'

Notice how much more useful these questions are than 'What do you mean by . . . ?'

## Imprecise verbs

The following questions recover specific information about the way a person is using a verb.

'My boss *annoyed* me.'
'*How exactly did he annoy you?*'

'Productivity is *falling.*'
'*How, specifically, is productivity falling?*'

'I am *frightened.*'
'*Exactly what is it that is frightening you?*'

## Verbs which have been turned into vague nouns

These are known as nominalisations – nouns which mean something to the speaker but whose meaning is unclear to others.

'I want *recognition.*'
'*How, specifically, do you want to be recognised?*'

'She wants a better *education*.'
'*What exactly does she mean by education?*'

'Job *satisfaction* is important to him.'
'*In what ways, precisely, does he want to feel satisfied?*'

These questions reveal the meaning of the verb by re-activating it and enabling us to understand the speaker's interpretation of the 'nominalisation'.

## Unspecified comparisons

The following questions will help you to discover the standard by which the comparison is being made.

'This is the *most useful* model.'
'*More useful than what, exactly?*' Or, '*In what specific ways is it more useful?*'

'She's the *best* person for the job.'
'*Better than whom, specifically?*'

'This product is *cheapest*.'
'*Cheaper than what, exactly?*'

## Apparent rules, limitations and generalisations

The following questions probe limits which are placed on actions or thoughts. They examine people's value judgements. They challenge perceived rules and exceptions.

'You *musn't* do it that way.'
'*What would happen if I did?*'

'We *should* always make sure that we keep a copy.'
'*What would happen if we didn't keep copies?*'

'We *must* get the financial report out by the 15th.'
'*What would happen if we were later than that?*'

'I *can't* do that.'
'*I can understand your difficulty but what exactly prevents you from doing it?*'

'We *never* promote people in their first two years.'
'*Was there ever a time when you did promote someone earlier than that?*'

'*Everybody* should seek further education.'
'*Everybody . . . ?*'

'That's *not possible.*'
'*What would have to happen to make it possible?*'

Use these questions with some care as they could cause trouble. Your boss says: 'You can't have an extra day off.' Responding with: 'What would happen if I did?' could well infuriate your boss. Try instead – 'What would have to happen for me to have that day off?' or 'May I ask what's preventing you from saying I can?' Notice what happens when you use rules, limitations and generalisation questions on yourself, to challenge your own preconceived ideas and thinking processes.

## When people's thinking distorts reality

The following questions explore and reform distortions in people's perception of the world. For example, a distortion is where X is assumed automatically to lead to Y; value judgements, rules and opinions in which the source of the assertion is missing; assuming you know what someone is thinking or feeling; belief that one person's action can cause another's emotional reaction, rather than simply inviting it.

'It's *wrong* to think like that.'
*'How do you know it is wrong?'*

'We can't buy a different policy *because* it will cost too much.'
*'How would having another policy cost you too much?'*

'People like that *annoy me.*'
*'How do people like that annoy you?'*

'That's professionally presented, *so* it's certain to be expensive.'
*'How does a professional presentation mean that it's certain to be expensive?'*

'You *don't understand* what I'm saying.'
*'What leads you to believe that I don't understand you?'*

## Tread carefully

The effect these questions may have on others can be alarming. You are asking them to see things from a new or different perspective. For some people this process can be both difficult and annoying. Think carefully about your motives – will the use of these questions clarify language to the advantage of both parties? If the words used by the other person are unimportant to the outcome of the dialogue – don't bother to use the PowerQuestion technique.

When you have developed your skills in PowerQuestioning and have been doing this subconsciously for a while, begin to notice what signs you get which let you know you are successfully distinguishing the other person's use of language and the right moment to use a PowerQuestion.

*When he saw the till receipt for more than £70,000, the manager asked to see the salesperson concerned.*

*'Chris, this is the biggest single sale ever made by one of our counter assistants. I want you to describe for me in detail, step by step, how you made the sale. What did the customer buy?'*

*'Twenty-five trout fishing hooks.'*

*'They're not £70,000.'*

*'I sold him some fishing line and reels, weights, wet and dry fishing flies and a rod. Obviously, he needed waders and waterproof clothing and a hat. I told him that it would be difficult carrying all that stuff so he would be better off with a permanent base to fish from. I sold him one of our prefabricated cabins. As the roads are pretty bad in the mountain regions, I convinced him to buy a four-wheel drive Jeep Cherokee. Oh, yes, then there was the boat and the trailer and the outboard motor.'*

*'This is amazing, Chris. You mean, this customer just came in asking for fish hooks and you sold him all these extras?'*

*'No, Mister Gresham. He didn't come in for fish hooks at all.'*

*'What did he come in for, then?'*

*'He just asked for directions to our maternity wear department, so I said, "You look like being in for a rather boring time. Have you tried trout fishing?"'*

## 4  The highest form of courtesy
### Listening with care and attention

Listening is a magnetic and strange thing, a creative force. The friends who listen to us are the ones we move towards. When we are listened to, properly listened to, it creates us, makes us unfold and expand. Listening is a hugely underrated skill. Although not taught at home or in schools, it is arguably *the* core communication skill, the foundation of all the others. If you are to become a Perfect Persuader, the value and importance of listening with care and curiosity cannot be stressed too much. We have two ears, but also eyes and a heart. When you use all three, your heightened sensory acuity will help you become a more accomplished listener, able to encourage others to unfold and expand. The deeper, more robust information you receive will in turn enable you to suggest accurate, appropriate and acceptable solutions. Watching others in social situations will show you that most people listen some of the time. The opposite of talking is not listening. For many people the opposite of talking is waiting – waiting to get back into the conversation, thinking out our next statement or argument; even at times looking away from the speaker, noticing our surroundings or – worst of all – listening to the conversation across the way.

# Becoming a good listener

There's nothing more frustrating and annoying than speaking to someone who's clearly not listening. Our brains become focused on 'why aren't they listening?' rather than on what we are saying. Our sentences become garbled, our arguments fuzzy, we forget crucial words.

It is easy to become known as a genuine listener; try following the suggestions below.

## Listen with your eyes

Never take your eyes off the person to whom you are listening. Even if they are not directing their speech at you it is still important to look at them. Give your full attention and use the sensory information you get back to assist your interpretation of what's being said. Don't worry about 'staring out' the speaker. You will notice that most speakers don't look directly at the listener all of the time. If they do have a direct gaze, you can be confident that they won't worry too much if you have a level gaze as well.

## Body language

Use your posture and gestures to signal that you are listening. There are no 'rules' to follow – just be natural. Many people find that leaning forward – towards the speaker – is preferable to leaning back or away. A hand cupped around the chin, forefinger vertically up the cheek and head tilted slightly will signal rapt attention. Tilt your head further to left or right and you will indicate your concern and empathy. Give plenty of nods and appropriate facial expressions to confirm you are listening. Strangely, if you started as a passive listener, by becoming *active* – showing clearly that you are hanging on to every word being said – you will hear, and see, so much more.

## Noises off

Given that many speakers do not look continuously at their listener, a few sounds and short phrases can enhance the listening process. Examples: 'I see'; 'Uh huh'; 'Oh really'; 'Did you?'; 'So what happened then?' Laughter or appropriate sounds suggesting amazement, sympathy, and so on, will encourage and propel the speaker during the short periods when they are not looking at you. This is how we behave when we are speaking on the telephone, to signal that we are still connected.

## Reflective questions and matching language patterns

Reflective questions are psychologically powerful signals that prove beyond doubt that you are listening carefully – it is impossible to use reflective questions without listening.

These questions spring from (reflect) previous information gained from the speaker's conversation content and contain the speaker's words, phrases, language patterns and even intonation.

Speaker: When the system broke down it caused enormous problems.
You: So how did you overcome the *enormous problems*?
Speaker: We decided to bring in consultants.
You: How successful were the *consultants* at sorting out the *problems*?

In this example, it is not necessary to interpret at this stage what are the 'problems', or who the 'consultants' are, or where they came from. Your speaker knows those answers, and that for the time being is sufficient. By using their descriptive terms you automatically tap into the speaker's way of thinking and seeing.

The effective listener will recognise that the speaker uses certain language patterns (for example: 'I'm really fed up with this guy') or technical terminology. Noticing this, the effective listener will use the same language in their responses: 'What is it that is making you *fed up with this guy*?'

## Listening with your heart

The truly empathic listener can feel what the speaker is feeling. This comes from consistently using sensory acuity to notice the facial signals which accompany speech, by studying the changes in skin colour, by observing the speaker's breathing rhythm, by noticing changes in voice volume and speed.

## Listening *can* be learned

Learn to become a great listener. It isn't difficult but demands consistency. There's nothing worse than being a good listener today and a half-hearted listener tomorrow. Set people's expectations that you will listen, and listen properly to what they tell you, and your success as a Perfect Persuader will rocket overnight. From today set yourself some listening outcomes:

- Begin to notice how you listen. What stimulates you to listen more actively? What distractions prevent you from concentrating? Do you use a particular style or type of listening? Do you listen differently to people you know or like? Is your approach different with customers? colleagues? management? partner?

What will you do from now on to improve your listening skills?

- Experiment with not listening! Notice the effect it has on others. Do this in face-to-face conversations as well as on the telephone. Notice also what takes place when you revert to active listening; what effect it has on the speaker.

- Practise matching your voice with other people. Without lapsing into mimicry, speak as they do – fast, slow, loud, soft. Notice their tone of voice and match it. Notice what happens to their voice when you alter your voice tone. Notice how your matching changes the way you listen and how you feel about the speaker.

- Be aware of the content of conversations. Notice the jargon and language patterns the other person uses. See what happens if you mismatch these patterns. What happens when you step into their map of reality by matching the patterns?

When others recognise you as a perfect listener they will come to you with issues that concern them. Your obvious respect for them will open many channels of persuasion.

> *The wise old owl lived in an oak;*
> *The more he saw the less he spoke;*
> *The less he spoke the more he heard:*
> *Why can't we all be like that bird?*

# 5 Something for everyone

*I love strawberries, but when I go fishing I bait my hook with worms – fishes' favourite food.*
Dale Carnegie, writer, 1888–1955

Probably the biggest single weakness demonstrated by salespeople is that they don't match the benefits of the proposition to the needs of the customer.

Recently, a friend called David wanted to change his car. For years he had been driving company cars, mainly Fords. Now self-employed he thought he should make some changes. One Saturday morning, David headed for the local Volvo showroom and was looking around when a salesperson approached him. The dialogue went something like this:

Salesperson: Good morning, my name is Alex. Are you looking for something specific or just seeing what we have to offer?

David: Hello, I'm David Smith. I want to change my car so thought I would come in and see what you have available.

Alex: Why don't you take a seat, Mister Smith and you can tell me a bit more about your requirements. By the way, would you like a coffee or would you prefer tea? (*Fetches coffee in thin plastic cups that take a good five minutes to drink as they are so hot to handle.*)

Alex: What sort of car do you drive at present, Mister Smith?

David: A two-litre Ford saloon, a company car.

Alex: I see. And what sort of driving do you use it for mainly? Is it city or country, motorways or smaller roads, business or pleasure?

David: Mainly business on motorways. I do about 40,000 kilometres a year. I also use the car for holidays.

Alex: I get the picture. Tell me, Mister Smith, how many passengers do you usually carry and where do you go on holiday?

David: It's usually my wife and two teenage children. We generally rent a property abroad, so we have a fairly full car.

Alex: And which is most important to you – safety or fuel consumption?

David: Definitely safety. I have the family to think about and I carry around a lot of bulky and valuable equipment. I claim petrol expenses on my company.

Alex: I see. How about reliability – how important is that to you?

David: Probably the most important single consideration. I am a self-employed consultant and have very strict deadlines to meet. I do not want to be worrying all the time about breaking down. I'd say reliability and safety are my chief concerns.

The conversation continued in this fashion for a little longer, then Alex suggested they look at a particular car.

Alex: I believe this is the car for you, Mister Smith. It's an estate, so you can easily load that bulky equipment. It also gives you plenty of extra space for those long trips abroad with the family. Safety and reliability are the hallmarks of Volvo, which are regarded by most people as the leaders in this field. As we recommend frequent servicing, this helps to avoid future problems as we replace parts before they become a problem.

This example shows how two persuasion skills can be put to work in conjunction with one another. The first is a detailed fact find which probes and analyses requirements (did you spot the values, the beliefs, the needs and the wants?). The second skill is showing how the benefits of the sales proposal dovetail with the needs.

## What's in it for me?

How many times have you been at a meeting or presentation where the speaker rambles on and on about specific details when all you want to know is 'What is in it for me?' The problem is simple. Most of us can get very worked up about an idea or a project. We live, sleep and eat it. So when the time comes to tell others all about it, we overdo the detail. I remember once buying a radio. It was just what I wanted but the sales assistant insisted on taking the back off the set in order to show me all the 'interesting' electronic components it contained. He was a fan of all things electronic; the shiny bits and bobs really excited his imagination. I could not fault his enthusiasm – it simply did not ignite mine. I couldn't care less about the innards. All I wanted to know was: 'Will it receive the BBC in South-east Asia? If so, I'll have it.'

This common problem can easily be corrected. At its core lies the blurred distinction between features of the item or idea, the benefits those features provide and any advantages it has when compared with alternatives.

# Benefits, features and advantages

Every time you attempt to influence or persuade someone you will be stressing benefits, features and advantages. You can't avoid it. They are the building blocks of your persuasive case. Each in its way is valuable. They all add credence to your message. But they do not carry the same value. If we scaled the three building blocks in order of value it would look like this:

1. Benefits – highly potent whenever they actually fulfil perceived needs and wants.

2. Features – potentially boring details; unnecessary information unless the other person requires proof or evidence or loves all the technical information.

3. Advantages – useful but possibly dangerous as they inevitably include comparisons with alternative courses of action.

To really understand the value and potency of benefits, advantages and features we need some definitions.

## Translate features into benefits

Imagine you are facilities manager for a medium-sized engineering company. Let's take a closer look at benefits, features and advantages and how each may be used to develop an appropriate argument with which to convince your directors.

At present, tea or coffee is brewed twice a day in a central kitchen. There is a hot-water boiler, a sink, cupboards for provisions and shelves where cups and mugs are stored. Each section (about eight workers) has a morning and afternoon break, staggered to avoid clashing with other sections. One person is allocated the task of making tea or coffee for his or her section for one week.

You have been approached by VivaVend, a vending machine company. They can see many flaws in your current system:

- time wasting (dispensing drinks; washing-up)

- unhygienic (cracked mugs; poor washing-up)

- dangerous (breakages)

- morale (workers tied down to fixed break times)

- money wasting (in terms of time spent; ingredients used; utensils).

VivaVend are proposing the installation of four suitably located vending machines. Each would dispense a variety of beverages, 24 hours a day. Drinks would be delivered in the familiar plastic cups, ribbed sides, conical, coffee-coloured.

Let's examine the eight main **features** of these plastic cups:

1. 1p per cup

2. 10 cm high

3. conical shape

4. made from plastic

5. coffee-coloured

6. ribbed sides

7. disposable

8. produced locally.

These eight features are technical aspects. Even if the directors do not agree with your proposals to install vending machines, these technical features will remain true of the plastic cups.

Only after agreeing to go ahead will the features become **benefits**. It is impossible to benefit from anything until you acquire it, use it, read it, see it – and so on. The problem with most sales people (and imperfect persuaders) is that they are so familiar with the features of their proposal that they forget to translate them into attractive benefits for the other person.

Knowing all the features of your proposition or idea is important. You may be asked to prove your claims, and features are a way of validating your conclusions – a form of proof. Even more important is the ability to avoid talking about them. The only thing that will ignite the other person's imagination is the answer to the age-old question: 'What's in it for me?' In other words, how will I benefit from your idea? How do the benefits dovetail with my perceived needs?

If you do need to mention features then also point out the attendant benefits in the same breath. For example: 'These cups are made from plastic (product feature) *which means that* they are more hygienic than mugs and will cut down sickness and absenteeism (benefit).' Or, 'These plastic cups are conical in shape (product feature) *which means that* they can be stacked and will save considerable storage space (benefit).'

Still in your role as facilities manager, imagine that you are preparing to present your case for vending machines at the weekly directors' meeting. The machine suppliers have given you a long list of features of which they are justifiably proud. You recognise that, while these will help back up your proposition in case technical detail or proof is required, they are also potentially boring. Exposure to too many features can easily lose an otherwise solid case. Take the list of features above and put at least two relative benefits alongside each.

Use this model next time you are preparing to influence change. List the features of your proposal then add the benefits and advantages. Note: this model will only work if you are familiar with the needs and wants of the person you are influencing. Don't fall into the trap of second-guessing them – find out first.

## The dangers of mentioning advantages

First of all – what do we mean by an 'advantage'? A thesaurus might put it like this: *advantage*, head start, lead, edge, upper hand, trump card, ace up one's sleeve, leverage, clout.

Your proposition includes additional features and benefits when compared to an alternative proposition. You are suggesting a new way of doing things, a different approach. But there is an alternative. Will the other person prefer the alternative? Is this something they are familiar with, happy with, comfortable with? Even if your proposal is cheaper, faster, easier, an improvement, smaller, larger, nearer, guaranteed, more accessible and more popular, there is no certainty that it will achieve universal acclaim.

Why not? It has so many advantages to offer, surely it cannot fail? There are several possible reasons:

1. They are happy with the present situation. 'Why change just for the sake of it? We might find ourselves going from the frying pan into the fire.' Perhaps there is some kind of 'deal' which obliges them to remain as they are.

2. They agree with everything you say, but everything you say contrasts rather too favourably with earlier decisions that they made. Why didn't they do what you are suggesting the first time around? What will their boss or partner think if they suddenly switch horses in midstream? Won't their judgement be called into question? 'Better to stay as we are, thanks all the same.'

3. Unconvinced of the final dividends. 'OK, so we'll save effort and worry – but for £45,000? No thanks!' Or, 'Sure the cost will rise if I don't make a decision to go ahead. All the more reason to stay as I am.'

4. Too much trouble. 'It's just not worth the trouble that change would involve.'

5. Sheer cussedness. 'OK, I realise you have some good points to make – but I just don't want to change. That's that. Sorry.'

The way in which you disclose your advantages can determine your eventual success. Phrases that may antagonise people include:

- 'I can't see why you persist with the old system when mine is so much better.'

- 'Just think of all the time you'll save.'

- 'That way of doing things is from the Dark Ages. You need to get up to speed, enter the twenty-first century.'

- 'Everyone else is doing it this way – you'll see the light sooner or later.'

Don't fall into the trap of thinking that these comments are so crass as to be laughable. I have heard every one of these statements made. Each is intended to shift the other person's perceptions, to encourage them to reconsider old beliefs. But all they succeed in producing is what psychologists call 'cognitive dissonance' – an even more determined attempt to rationalise and support old ideas. In other words: 'I know what you say makes sense but I'll stick with what I've got, if you don't mind.'

## How to present advantages

Even if your proposition provides important advantages, take care how you 'sell' them. A clumsy approach may create cognitive dissonance. Put yourself in the other person's shoes. Ask yourself: how would I react to these apparent advantages? Think carefully before you present the advantages of your ideas. You will be making comparisons with other possible solutions, including 'do nothing'. If you are to avoid cognitive dissonance setting in, you must phrase your advantage statements very carefully. Here are some suggestions you might like to try next time you need to be more successful at convincing someone of the advantages of your proposal. You will notice that both questions force the other person to examine the possibilities of beneficial success.

- 'If you were to save even more time by doing it this way, how exactly might that benefit your department?'

- 'What would have to happen for you to test my claims over a three-month period in order to check for yourselves that the additional savings are worth having?'

A further method of proving advantages is by encouraging others to check the validity of your assertions. 'Jo was sceptical of the advantages so I suggested she called Sam to verify. Why not give Jo a call yourself?'

*An animal-feed salesman is late for his appointment at Giles Farm. He is roaring down a lane at 100 k.p.h. when he is overtaken by a chicken with three legs. He arrives at the farm and asks Mr Giles to explain.*

*'Well,' says Giles, 'we raise three-legged chickens because I like a leg, so does my wife, and my son too. We used to kill two chickens*

*which was a waste, so we decided to breed three-legged chickens so each of us would get a drumstick.'*

*'I can see the advantages, but tell me, what do they taste like?' asks the salesman.*

*'Dunno. We've never been able to catch one.'*

# 6 It's good to get along
## Building rapport and developing trust

Aristotle said that when man is in good health and prosperous, he enjoys the company of his friends; in times of trouble he is in need of them; in old age, when his body is weak, he is assisted by them. The Perfect Persuader understands and relies on the power of relationships. Social and business networking is a must. In the same way that people need people – people also 'buy' people.

Close to my home there are two pubs. One sells very good beers and cider, the other is 'tied' to a brewer and obliged to sell that brewer's proprietary brands. The people who run the tied house are generous, helpful and very friendly – which is why I drink there, rather than at the pub which sells the better beer. So what is it that influences my decision? Good beer, or the people who run the pub? Most of us base decisions of this sort on the people factor. If we like the people, we'll buy. If we don't like the people and can buy just as conveniently elsewhere – forget it. Even if it causes us some inconvenience we will find someone we *do* like – and give them the business.

So, if people do buy people, how easy will it be to isolate those people factors that may be important when trying to persuade others? It is at once easy and difficult. Easy because all of us are able to interact with some people better than others. Difficult because most of us do not bother to analyse the reasons why we do or don't have a harmonious relationship. If we did stop for a moment to study our evaluative processes we would discover that it all reduces to one thing – rapport.

Rapport is the lubricant of all human communication. It is the ultimate influencing skill, more important than our knowledge of our subject, awareness of our 'market', or ability to persuade. Good rapport oils the wheels of the many communications we have with other human beings. From the moment we leave our bed to the time our head hits the pillow once more, most of us are in almost perpetual contact with other people. And, without rapport to smooth the interface of daily communication, many potential opportunities to persuade and influence can be lost.

It has been calculated that the average person has no more than a dozen friends on earth. Not acquaintances – real friends. Don't believe it? Stop now, find a piece of paper and start listing your friends. (What is a friend? A single soul dwelling in two bodies. Someone on whom you could rely totally in times of real crisis; someone who would lend you money and give you space in their home for an indefinite period. Someone who would share their bathwater??) How did you do? If you listed more than nine, count yourself lucky – you are doing pretty well for friends in your life. (A recent poll [Gallup, 2003] showed that on average Americans claimed nine close friends.)

Friends are usually those people with whom you have the greatest rapport. A harmonious relationship where you immediately feel comfortable. No special behaviour is required from you or them. No posturing, or wariness is necessary – every time you meet one another you both dive deep into an engaging and enduring partnership with ease and joy. Time has worn away the rough edges of your early relationship. Like favourite clothes, or a comfortable chair, your real friendships require no 'wearing in' period.

Wouldn't it be great if you could slip as easily into all your social and business relationships? Just think how rich you would be – materially and spiritually – if all the people you have to persuade, convince, influence and interact with were as comfortable to be with as your own friends. It is possible to develop early and long-lasting rapport with others with remarkably little effort. All you need to do is understand exactly what you are doing now which makes some personal relationships so successful and transfer these natural skills to all other relationships. A complete awareness of your own natural social skills will give you the power to transfer these skills straight into any social or business relationship. Before we break down these instinctive techniques of yours into digestible chunks for further learning, let's examine some basic areas of business (and social) communication which may require the lubrication of rapport. It is easier to influence change in others if you:

- are able to form strong, long-lasting relationships easily and quickly

- understand how your personality dovetails with others

- are aware of and develop elementary non-verbal communication skills.

## Strong relationships: society's cement

How many times have you walked into a room full of strangers and made immediate judgements about them? Which one do I like? Who am I most likely to feel comfortable with? Who is the most desirable or interesting-looking person here? My guess is – most of us do this, most of the time. It's only human, after all. We make decisions about the rest of humanity based on our unerring ability to read people like a book!

At first, all goes according to plan. We circle around one another forming the first steps in the dance of rapport. Perhaps the other person knows the same moves – and, for a while, we circle together in a simple two-step. But then the tune changes or others want to join in. We discover that our first impression was incorrect. Maybe just slightly wrong; sometimes totally wrong.

This is a common phenomenon. The reason we make many misjudgements about other people is because, in the formation phase of a relationship, people often make allowances for each other in order to develop the relationship faster. Example: you have just met someone for the first time. You strike up a conversation and soon discover you like this person. They seem to like your company, too. You chat about that play you both saw on TV last night – the play you thought was the best you have seen for a long time. It turns out that your new acquaintance thought the play was poorly written and badly acted. 'Yes,' you find yourself half agreeing, 'it wasn't that well acted and maybe the writing was a little flat at times.'

Only moments into the relationship and you have already prepared to tone down some beliefs and attitudes. You are modifying your more radical ideas, suppressing some of your wilder thoughts. It is quite common for people to do this – in order to keep the relationship on track during its delicate formation phase. But, do you always do this with people at work or new neighbours? Many people believe it is more important to have good relationships with people outside work than in business. Why should we have to adjust our cherished beliefs in front of this new customer? After all, we probably wouldn't choose to be with them in a social situation. The answer to this common dilemma is easy. You need never again compromise your position.

Suppose others say something you don't agree with – a political judgement, perhaps, or some negative comment about a third person. In future, instead of stating your case and risking conflict in the early formation phase of the relationship, learn to see things always from their point of view.

## The more points of view you have, the better

The person in any complex communication who has the greatest variety of possible viewpoints is in a better position to control the dialogue. To understand this concept, take as an example a typical home central heating system. A big, powerful boiler fired by gas, perhaps; plenty of radiators linked by a lengthy network of copper tubing; a hot-water tank, one or two heated towel rails. What controls the system? The size of each radiator? The length of piping? The gas pressure? None of these controls the system. The thermostat controls it. The smallest, but most flexible 'thinking' part of the entire system is in charge.

Try looking at things from different points of view:

1. our own point of view

2. the other person's viewpoint

3. imagining how an outsider might see things.

It is all too easy to see things solely from our own point of view. From now on, you may find yourself saying things such as: 'I can understand why you think that, Mister Garrison.' 'Hmmm. I see your point of view.' 'Yes, that's understandable, Nichola.' When you do this, you will not be compromising – you will be empathising.

It also helps to avoid saying 'Yes – but'. From now on, say 'Yes

– AND'. Every time you use the word 'but', you immediately indicate that you do not mean 'yes' at all. What you really mean is 'NO!'

Later, when you get to know a person better, you can and possibly should, come off the fence and show your true colours. But avoid the temptation in the early formation phase, especially in a business relationship.

All long-term relationships go through three, and sometimes four, distinct phases:

- formation

- development

- consolidation and further development on new levels of understanding

- breakdown.

As a flexible persuader you will naturally want to form strong relationships by reaching phase three, consolidation, as soon as you can – and keep the relationship there for as long as possible, without ever reaching the breakdown phase.


## Maps of reality: our unique view of the world

Persuasion is largely about words: the words used to persuade or influence and the way in which the recipient interprets them. It sounds straightforward enough but there is a major snag. As I mentioned previously, we all see the world from a different perspective. As human beings, we can never know reality. The real world is a highly complex, changing environment and to make sense of it we simplify it to give it meaning. We filter and minimise the information that we see and hear and sense to make it fit our preconceived view of the world. We can only know our individual, personal perceptions of reality.

In order to recall our influences, thoughts, ideas, memories and perceived truths, we create a 'map' of reality as we see it. But maps are not the territory they describe. They are selective and distort reality by leaving out, or only giving, certain pieces of information. In the same way, when we create our personal map of reality we filter the information we receive. We attend to those aspects that interest us, and ignore or leave out those that do not. These filters determine our world, as we know it. It is not reality that can limit or empower us, but rather our map of reality. As Kahlil Gibran said: 'We choose our joys and sorrows long before we experience them.'

If a geologist, an artist and a botanist walked through natural woodland, they would record different experiences. What one noticed, the others might not see at all, or decide to ignore. Similarly, how we see or ignore information determines the sort of world we live in. The same world can be to one person exciting, vibrant and endlessly stimulating. To another, it may seem dull, uninspiring, samey. Because two people can interpret the same world so differently, the words we choose to describe that world can take on quite different meanings.

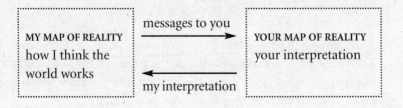

It's easy to see how conversations, in particular persuasive conversations, can go awry. Take the word 'book'. Books come in all shapes and sizes but remain broadly the same. But how about words such as 'activity' or 'motivation' or 'education'? The meaning of communication is the response it gets; it's our responsibility to get it as 'right' as we want it to be. The best possible way of achieving this is to:

- Step inside the other person's 'reality', stay there, and get to know it.

- Listen carefully and differentiate *form* from *content*.

- Use their language and language patterns.

- Avoid critical analysis of their reality. It is what they believe it to be.

Take this dialogue as an example:

Persuader: What do you believe to be the most important element in bringing up children?
Recipient: Their education.
Persuader: How do you believe that today's children should be *educated*?
Recipient: I think there should be more focus on vocational education.
Persuader: In what ways do you think vocational education could be *more focused*?

This example illustrates two important techniques. The first shows how the word 'education' means something specific to the recipient but is meaningless to the persuader. So the persuader reactivates the noun 'education' by turning it into the verb 'educated'.

The second technique is to stay inside the recipient's map of reality by simply using their words and phrases. For example: *focus*. It is not always necessary to understand what a word or phrase means. Nor do you have to agree with what others are saying. There is a clear difference between empathy and sympathy. Empathy is putting yourself into someone else's shoes; sympathy is walking off in them.

# Business relationships

The formation of early business relationships is quite easy. All you have to do is follow two rules: remain flexible and avoid 'Yes – but . . . ' More work, much more effort, is required if you are to move easily into the development and consolidation phases of your new relationship.

Earlier, we showed how to transfer natural social skills into the formation phase of a new relationship. Now you need to understand precisely what skills you employ which make your personal relationships flourish and survive the test of time. These skills, too, can be developed within all business relationships. Although most of us discover a variety of ways which help us to rub along with others, there are three principle techniques for the development and consolidation of your relationships:

- by meeting frequently

- by being prepared to self-disclose

- through discovering things you have in common.

## Meeting frequently

My wife and I have some very good friends who live on the other side of the country, a six-hour drive away. We don't see one another very often – perhaps once or twice a year, at most. Last time we met, Jane and Pete observed how our relationship was always 'so easy to pick up where we left off last time. We have a seamless conversation which carries on, uninterrupted, down the years.' However, the reality is very different. Our relationship has actually stood still.

Each of us has changed over the years. Events, growth and development, even death have all had an impact on our separate lives. When we meet on one of our infrequent encounters, these influential events have not been shared – we are largely unaware of how each of our lives has been affected in the intervening time we have spent apart. We have not grown alongside one another. We have increasingly less in common. We lead separate existences. The couple we travel all that distance to see have become different people. Our relationship is teetering on the edge of breakdown. We have literally grown apart. Clearly, the more opportunity you have to meet others the greater will be the chances of developing a lasting relationship. You will constantly be tuned in to their ever-changing needs, attitudes and beliefs; better able to react swiftly to these altered circumstances with appropriate suggestions. Familiarity need not necessarily breed contempt. Well-adjusted adults tend to be able to adapt well to one another.

One of my clients, a life insurance company, sells their products through a broker network. Recently, I was chatting to one of their brokers, tied exclusively to my client, and asked her, 'What made you choose Osborne Life?' Without hesitation she replied, 'Gary. He was the reason I chose Osborne.' Intrigued, I quizzed her further. 'So what was it Gary did that impressed you most?' The broker paused, then smiled widely. 'It wasn't what he did as much as what he didn't do. He didn't give up.' She went on: 'The first time I met him, I was quite rude to him and told him to leave my office. The second time, he stayed a bit longer and we chatted for a while. Not about Osborne Life Assurance – about my business, the economy and so on. We discovered we both played squash at the same sports centre. We knew some of the same people. But I still told him not to bother me further as I was quite happy with the business arrangement I had with another life assurance company.'

I gently pushed her for more information. 'He obviously didn't stay away?' 'No,' she replied, 'he didn't.' Apparently, two weeks later she went into her outer office and discovered Gary sitting there, talking to a clerical assistant. It seems that Gary had discovered the assistant was unsure of a recent change in financial services legislation and he was talking her through it. Noticing this, the broker asked him to step inside her office for a chat. 'Later, Gary told me that he was frightened that I was about to reprimand him for pestering my staff. Instead, we talked in detail about the Finance Services Act, his sales philosophy and, inevitably, Osborne Life Assurance. The rest is history. When I decided to switch companies, I didn't buy Osborne Life Assurance – I bought Gary.'

So, persistence does pay off, after all. The relationship consolidates, and influencing others becomes quite natural and no pressure is needed.

## Disclosing information

Most of us like people who are like ourselves. We swarm, flock and group together by type, background, interests, beliefs, gender, work, and so on. But how do we find out enough about other people to decide whether we want to be in their company in the first place?

The answer is, we consciously disclose information. Most developing relationships reach a point at which one or other party feels the urge to reveal aspects of their life or themselves to the other person. This can happen verbally, as in: 'I'm off on holiday at the end of the week,' which invites the response, 'Oh, really? Where are you going?' More subtly, one statement tucked into another: 'When I worked in the retail trade . . . ' can tempt the listener to ask: 'I didn't know you were in retailing. When was that . . . ?'

Perhaps you wear a special tie (old school?) or a badge or pin which shows you are a member of a club, or have some special interest or religious belief. If so, you are disclosing information about yourself. Remember – most people only self-disclose because they want you to pick up on what they have said or indicated. With few exceptions, you should *always* follow through self-disclosure. And by noticing self-disclosure in the future, picking up on it you will discover that it frequently leads on to . . .

## Knowing me, knowing you

We have already learned that many people feel an affiliation with others who are in some way like themselves. This is a small part of what is known as 'matching'. It is rare for people who have little in common to congregate in one another's company for long. Mutual interests, ideas, values and beliefs are the warp and weft of social interaction and they help bind us to one another. Easy enough in social circles but far more difficult when you find yourself confronted by a customer with a big budget – with whom you have absolutely nothing in common.

Because matching can be social or economic, achieved through outlook, education or background, it is rare for two human beings to avoid the compulsion to discover similarities about themselves. All of us love creating little compartments into which we can pop other people. Following some early self-disclosure, a typical matching conversation might go something like this:

You: You were saying that you are off for a long weekend in the Lake District. Do you manage to get away from the business very often?

Them: No – this is the first time for about a year. Our daughter was born last March, so we feel we can get out and about a bit more now.

You: We have a six-month-old son and know the feeling. Whereabouts in the Lake District are you staying?

Them: Near Ullswater – do you know it?

You: Yes, very well. A neighbour of ours has a cottage which she lets to one or two acquaintances.

Them: I wouldn't mind her telephone number sometime – we'd be very interested in renting a decent place next year.

All this may sound unrealistic and a bit contrived but, if you look back on conversations you have had with near strangers, real life is frequently more extraordinary than any conversation I could dream up. Recently, I was flying from London to Kuala Lumpur, via Singapore. On the London–Singapore leg of the journey, I sat next to a woman who was employed by a client of mine in the UK. Naturally, we chatted a lot and found that we had much in common and, of course, discovered that we had several mutual acquaintances through her job. On the next leg of my journey, I sat beside a man who turned out to be the Hong Kong vice-president of one of the world's largest insurance groups. After only a few minutes' conversation, and employing the notion of Six Degrees of Separation*, we discovered we had a mutual friend

---

* *Six Degrees of Separation* refers to the belief that if a person is one step away from each person they know and two steps away from each person who is known by one of the people they know, then we are all no more than six 'steps' away from each person on Earth.

who worked for another insurance company. I have since contacted his friend and started a business correspondence with the vice-president.

Small world? Certainly, it is. What are the chances, firstly of either of these people being aboard the same two aircraft that I am on, and secondly of me sitting next to both of them? The answer, of course, is: I would never have known if I hadn't got into conversation.

# 7 Silent messages
## Reading body language

*I speak two languages – Body and English.*
Mae West, actress, 1893–1980

The 2008 televised presidential debates between Senator John McCain and Senator Barack Obama say more about the impact of non-verbal communication or body language than any training film ever could. Those who heard the debates on radio, or who read transcripts in their newspaper, felt McCain performed far better than Obama. People watching the debates live on TV felt differently. Their interpretation of Obama's performance was enhanced and changed through seeing the body language signals that accompanied his words and voice tone. ('In fact, I think McCain won the debate on radio. But I thought Obama won the debate on television. The visual was the key for television . . . ' Source: www.npr.org)

Much has been written about the interpretation and use of body language in persuasive communication. I do not intend to cover body language in detail – it is sufficient to emphasise its importance and to highlight one or two points. In the last two decades, research in British and American universities has demonstrated that the non-verbal components of communication play a far more important role than was previously recognised. Further research has suggested the non-verbal aspect outweighs the verbal in both accuracy and validity. Body language and voice tonality have an enormous influence on anyone listening to us. Unfortunately, there is little we can do quickly to correct wrong impressions, once they have developed. We all know how difficult it is to shake off old-established negative feelings we may harbour about another person.

Face-to-face communication is always much more than the words we say, as it does not operate in a vacuum. The words and voice tones we choose are always accompanied by complementary body movements – posture and gestures. Subconscious and sublimated thoughts and feelings are openly expressed within the postures and gestures that accompany our words. People with good sensory acuity and empathy will pick up these unconscious signals and draw valid and useful conclusions from them. Women seem particularly sensitive to these subliminal personal messages. Recent studies at Oxford University and in the USA have shown women appear to be more tuned in to non-verbal communication signals than their male counterparts. (Victor Hugo once said that while men have foresight, women have insight.)

Being more aware of your non-verbal behaviour and that of others results in more effective when influencing communication – both ways. For the purposes of persuasion we need to remember one simple principle: *meaningful interpretation of body language can only be made from gesture clusters.*

A gesture cluster is a set of related movements – body posture, hands and arms, feet, head as well as facial expression. Before embarking on your persuasive communication, consider, how you want to be seen by the other person. Ask yourself a few questions about the way you want to appear:

- confident?

- relaxed?

- dynamic?

- controlled?

- enthusiastic?

- honest?

Imagine you have an important meeting with a person who you wish to influence in some way. You have their undivided attention for half an hour.

- What impression of you would you like this person to take away?

- How will you control and use your body posture in order to emphasise how you want to be seen?

- How will you control your gestures?

- What gestures would be seen as appropriate?

- What gestures will seem inappropriate?

- How and where will you sit or stand?

- How will you control and use your facial expressions?

Your non-verbal communication supports and sustains your message. Be sure it is the message you want to give. But don't spend so much time concentrating on your own non-verbal signals that you forget about the other person.

## Don't take that tone with me!

A few years ago my son was confronted by his grandmother. Imagine the scene. Elderly figure of authority standing over small boy, wagging her finger. There is a frown on her face, she clearly means business.

'You are a naughty little boy, aren't you?'

'Yes,' says Sam, grinning up at her. She laughs and ruffles his hair.

What exactly is going on here? How could he misinterpret her reprimand? How did he get away with it? When we read Grandma's words we can't hear the tone of voice she adopted. She had a laugh, a lilt in her voice. The end of the sentence lifted and indicated her approval and pleasure at her 'naughty' grandson. Communication is so much more than the words we speak. These form only a very small part of our expressiveness as human beings. For instance, research suggests only 7 per cent of our impact is determined by what we say. The other 93 per cent of our message is made up of body language (55 per cent) and the tone of our voice (38 per cent). Make sure your body language and tone of voice both correctly underpin the influencing message you want to convey.

## Observing the reaction to our message

How often have you met a friend and been able to notice before either of you has said a word exactly how they are feeling? Perhaps you don't know why they feel that way, just that they do. 'It was written all over her face.' 'If looks could kill.' These are familiar expressions which acknowledge the power of sensory awareness. Our internal responses are reflected in our external behaviour. Some people are better than others at gaining information this way. For some it represents a completely new channel of communication. But beware – it can be dangerous to jump to conclusions. I have a friend who walks about with a permanent look of worry on his face. When I first met him I noticed this and would often ask: 'Are you feeling all right? Is there anything I can do to help?' He would usually respond with surprise, saying there was nothing wrong. After a while I began to realise this was the case – he just *looked* worried.

Notice how others respond to your influence, log as much data as you are able, then notice it a second and third time. When you are confident your assessments are accurate you can proceed with more certainty. Heightening your natural skills will help you predict with greater accuracy how others might respond to your suggestions. As soon as you are skilled at predicting the likely response, you can begin to choose the words which will achieve that response.

Whenever we communicate with other people we obtain a reaction. Even if they say nothing and walk away from us, that is a reaction. One of the Perfect Persuader's most invaluable skills is 'sensory acuity' – the ability to use all our senses to read the reactions produced from our messages to others. If we notice a positive reaction, this will encourage us further. If the reaction is not what we want, we alter our approach until we achieve the desired reaction.

## The eyes have it . . .

We all know when people are lying (or modifying the truth) they will avoid looking at us. Or, because they know this themselves, they will spend the whole time staring fixedly at our eyes saying: 'No, honestly . . . really . . . that's the truth' – and we still know they are lying.

When you are chatting with a friend or colleague, begin to notice what happens to the micro-muscles which cluster around their eyes. Notice how the 'bags' will puff up when they genuinely smile and laugh. How their eyes narrow when they are puzzling over what you just said. How their pupils dilate with pleasure or desire.

## ... and so does the mouth

Surrounded by numerous tiny muscles, the mouth is a positive goldmine of additional information providing invaluable clues to people's responses. Notice how people will contrive to hide their mouth whenever they are distorting the truth. They may do this in a wholehearted fashion, covering their mouth with their entire hand. Or perhaps it is a subtle touch of the end of their nose with the top of their forefinger – blink and you'll miss it.

Watch how a mouth contracts or expands with passing emotions. In particular, observe the lower lip which most people find almost impossible to control when emotions course through the rest of their body. The lower lip is a great giveaway, tightening perhaps with doubt or fear, expanding and filling out with delight, pleasure or surprise, trembling with sadness or remorse, moistening with desire.

## I blush to think about it

Notice changes in flesh tone. Facial colouration often changes with stress. It may be the only outward sign that the other person is feeling stressed. Some people blush at the drop of a hat and this may signify nothing at all. It is possible to go white with fear, as the blood drains rapidly from the face. Watch for minute changes in skin colour. Look for patches or portions that change – the forehead may stay pale while cheeks, chin or even neck become redder in patches.

## Stopping for breath

Have you ever given a speech or attended a difficult interview? Were you aware of the way these stressful circumstances affected your breathing? Probably it came higher up your chest, shallower, faster. When you are relaxed, breathing becomes calmer and slower, from the lower abdomen.

Two things you can be sure of: one – different people breathe in different ways at different moments; two – any noticeable shift in breathing will suggest a change in the way that person is thinking or feeling.

How can the Perfect Persuader use this information? Try this experiment: next time you are with someone who is familiar to you (partner, colleague, boss), make a series of proposals to them. For example: 'Shall we go out tonight?' 'How about seeing a film?' 'Why don't we see the new Spielberg which is on at the Odeon?' – anything reasonably within the normal scope of conversation with this individual. Each time you make a suggestion, notice their physical response.

Are the physical signals you notice congruent with the verbal responses? What are those physical signals?

- eye movements

- lower lip changes

- skin colour changes

- changes in breathing

- foot moving up and down, or side to side.

Later, using a different set of suggestions, run the exercise again with the same person. This time, how accurately are you able to predict their physical or verbal responses? How does this affect the ways in which you change your tactics? To be certain your calibrations are accurate, run the exercise at least one more time (each person's responses will be different, so you will need to run it separately for different individuals).

## You are what you wear

Throughout the world clothing is used for modesty, comfort and display. It tells the society in which we live and work a lot about us. We make conscious daily decisions about the messages we want to project through our garments. Just as voice tone, posture and gesture underscore our influencing messages, so too does the clothing we choose to wear. It can heavily influence the way in which we are seen by others and the way in which our messages are received.

A salesman attending one of my training seminars told an interesting story. It seems whenever he left the office to sell he had with him three changes of clothing that he switched to match the person or organisation to whom he was selling. How did he do this? (*Where* did he do it?) Outfit one was a grey suit. He would substitute the suit jacket for either a blazer (outfit two) or a leather jacket (outfit three). His job was to sell newspaper advertising to a wide variety of businesses – smart offices, advertising agencies, run-down backstreet car lots. By providing himself with several dress options, he was expanding his opportunities to match the people to whom he sold.

But be careful – too much flexibility can work against you. Recently I was contacted by a company specialising in rendering the outside walls of houses. Coincidentally, I had been experiencing serious dampness in the front wall of the old house I live in, so I was open to any suggestions which might solve this problem. The company made an appointment for their surveyor to investigate, report back on his findings and recommend a solution.

That evening a van drew up outside the house and the surveyor knocked on the door. He was a middle-aged man, dressed in a dark grey boiler suit. He carried a metal case in one hand and introduced himself as the chief surveyor of the Such And Such Rendering Company. I let him in and chatted for a while about the problems I had been experiencing. He listened carefully, made a few notes and asked if he could give the outer wall a thorough inspection. He left me looking at a video of his company's innovative rendering technique. As I dutifully watched the short film I could hear the surveyor outside, tapping away at the wall. When he had finished, he sat down and quietly and confidently talked me through his findings and the technicalities of his proposed solution. I was impressed. He was serious, just technical enough, and looked the part. He left, saying he would call back the next day and give me a written quotation.

The following evening promptly at seven o'clock he arrived. No grey boiler suit, no metal box, not even a van. He was driving a smart new red car, carried a bulging briefcase and wore an expensive-looking dark suit with a loud silk tie and very shiny shoes. His whole approach was different. As he turned on the charm, the sales talk and eventually the pressure, it became very obvious that yesterday's 'surveyor' had become today's salesman. The quiet, serious man I had trusted 24 hours previously had disappeared. It was Dr Jekyll and Mr Hyde all over again and I could not wait to be rid of Mr Hyde.

Think about what you will wear when you next attempt to influence others. Ask yourself these questions:

- What clothing is likely to be considered inappropriate by the other person?

- What clothing is the most appropriate for the circumstances and the message I need to convey?

- What clothing will the other person or people be wearing?

- To what extent do I need to conform to their style of clothing?

- Should I ignore them and simply wear what I would like to wear?

It is impossible to wear clothing without sending social signals. Every outfit tells a story.


## Walking the talk

Have you ever noticed that sometimes spoken words do not appear to tally with the body language you are observing? Perhaps the other person is looking particularly relaxed, lolling back in a comfortable chair, uttering words like: 'This is *really* important. It is *essential* we do something about it – right away!' Clearly, the speaker is just saying the words – words which do not seem to underline the urgency they are stressing. They look far too relaxed to want to do anything much. What you are noticing here is a lack of congruity. It is interesting that when there are confused messages coming across, most people read the body language and do not believe the actual words spoken.

Beware – lack of congruity can weaken your own messages. How often have you found yourself extolling the virtues of some idea just because your manager or partner told you to – not because you actually believed what you were asked to say? Chances are your body language, your non-verbal signals, will give you away.

As a general rule, the more familiar you are with a person the more likely you are to be tuned in to their non-verbal signals. Have you ever wondered why it is a dog will know well in advance it is time for the evening walk? A standard pattern of behaviour has built up over time; the dog becomes aware of certain signals which always culminate in him being taken out. Like Pavlov's dogs, he salivates before the event takes place. Anyone who lives, or works, with another person for any length of time begins to find they are often one jump ahead of the other person's behaviour, thoughts and comments. For instance, I can always tell when an old friend is worrying about something. They have a habit of cupping their chin in their hand. Even at some distance, my sensory acuity is sufficiently tuned in to my friend's characteristic body language patterns.

## Beware of the single gesture trap

All language is full of ambiguities; one word alone can take on many different meanings. For example, the word 'fly' can be interpreted in over a dozen different ways. Taken out of context, a single word can be meaningless – other words are needed in order to provide a robust context for interpretation. In the same way, hasty analysis of non-verbal communication offers plenty of opportunity for misjudgement. A simple shrug of the shoulder can mean many things: resignation/don't care/don't know. When someone tugs slowly at their ear lobe, does this mean they are racked with self-doubt – or does their ear lobe itch? In order correctly to interpret the signals we observe, we must first look for more supporting signals – a 'cluster'.

When you are seated listening to someone, a typical cluster of your body language signals might consist of:

- leaning slightly forward in the chair
- hand/fingers grouped around chin
- head tilted slightly to the left
- a narrowing of the eyes
- good eye contact
- slow nods of the head.

This cluster of signals could suggest you are listening intently (*leaning forward/eye contact/eyes narrowing*), evaluating what they say (*fingers grouped around chin*), agreeing with them or their points (*head tilted/slow nods).*

## Spot the difference

Some people are often so wrapped up in what they are saying, so in love with their own voice, they fail to notice the changes in body language which are unfolding before them.

A colleague who started off looking alert, interested and keen slowly reveals they are not so enthusiastic after all. A forward-leaning person with good eye contact gradually becomes slouched, fidgety and awkward, no longer giving good eye contact but taking furtive peeks at their watch. Worse still, it is possible to overlook the person who starts off appearing as if they are not in the least bit interested then slowly changes posture and gesture, suggesting their level of interest has increased. Think about the number of people you know who miss your signals, even though they are taking place right under their noses.

Next time you need to influence others you may notice your senses are more tuned in to what is going on around you. You may take in the other person's initial posture and register this in your memory, so even small changes are easily noticed. Equally, developing and maintaining strong and effective body language will help you establish an immediate rapport with others, signalling confidence in your message.

# 8 Who do you think you are?
## All about personality styles

*What you are sounds so loudly in my ears that I cannot hear what you say.*
Ralph Waldo Emerson, philosopher, 1803–82

Interacting with other people forms a large part of the social fabric of everyday life. Our ability to conform to social expectations is one of the factors taken into account whenever we try to persuade others. As soon as we are old enough we are taught 'rules' by our parents and teachers. These appear to be designed to influence the way in which others will react towards ourselves. From the very beginning, our earliest transactions with the rest of humanity illustrate just how anxious we are to convince everyone that we are socially competent and therefore somehow 'right' to be with. Some of these 'rules' could be:

- It is rude to stare at strangers.

- You mustn't speak before you are spoken to.

- It is wrong to answer back.

- Always respect your elders and betters.

- Keep your room tidy at all times.

- Children should be seen but not heard.

Conversation whether business or social is an intricate skill. Special verbal and interactive skills are needed if we are to make friends and influence people. If we fail to master conversational strategies and tactics across a wide range of relationships, we inevitably weaken our power to influence others. Obviously, it is easier to convince people with whom we get on or have something in common. The difficulty arises when we meet people who have personalities with which we find it difficult to relate.

Recently a colleague had to meet a new training manager, a man taking over the role from someone she had worked with for several years. She had always got on very well with the old training manager. He was a rather dry and elderly gentleman with not much of a sense of humour, but my colleague and he saw eye to eye and worked well together. The new appointee was very different. Apart from a keen sense of fun, he brought an intellectual mind to his work. He was younger and more creative and innovative. Despite two very different personalities, my colleague managed to interact well with both men. She carefully nurtured both relationships. She did not pretend to be anyone other than herself, but did take care which aspects of her personality were on show at any one time. With Martin, the younger man, she was more jolly and fun to be with. They shared a lot of laughs and bounced many workable, creative ideas off one another. Meanwhile, she admired Ted, the older man, for his careful and dedicated approach to the job. He was slow and invariably took the traditional path but, in his slightly pedantic way, managed to run an extremely efficient department.

One day the inevitable took place. Martin suggested that the three meet together to discuss the year ahead. My colleague's heart sank. This would be the first time she had met both men together. The thought of being a 'pig in the middle' of these two was daunting. It would mean that she would be forced to reveal aspects of her personality that she had spent time shielding from both. It was a difficult meeting and she survived – but only just. The problem lay in the fact that the two relationships had flourished apart. If my colleague had worked jointly with both men, I expect her behaviour would have been more even and appealing to both personalities. There is no such thing as a *right* or *wrong* personality. Whatever our personality, it will work both for and against us and is interdependent on the personalities of others. Anyone with an ounce of empathy will take care to adapt their behaviour to suit both circumstances and people. A couple of years ago in the space of two weeks I attended a funeral, a wedding in France and a christening. Needless to say, I behaved quite differently on each occasion. I dressed differently, spoke in a different manner and tone, and said different things – each of them appropriate to the situation.

## How to be a chameleon

- Think of a person with whom you have a good relationship – someone in whose company you feel relaxed and comfortable. Describe how you feel towards them.

- Now recall someone with whom you do not have a good relationship. Every time you see or hear this person your heart sinks. They make you feel and act in a different manner. Describe how you typically behave towards this person.

- What are the main differences in your behaviour which make you a chameleon?

### Jung's pairs of behaviour

Much of our understanding of human behaviour stems from the work of Carl Jung (1875–1961), the founder of analytical psychology. Jung found there are recognised and repeated patterns in our behaviour. These patterns of habitual behaviour stem from our upbringing and development at home, in school and in society; they are developed early and can become quite difficult – though not impossible – to change. Because we all possess our own set of preferred behaviours we can easily become attracted to certain types of people, organisations and interests. At the same time we may make decisions, often unconsciously, to reject some people and groups in society. These decisions reflect our ingrained understanding of those personality characteristics that appear to mesh best, or conflict the most, with our own.

Jung's research identified four pairs of behaviour and found that most of us engage with only one of each pair to a greater or lesser extent. He also found that almost all the people he analysed had also developed one of these paired traits in preference to the other. Each trait is useful for certain tasks/jobs/professions but often creates problems with other tasks.

Carl Jung described his four pairs of personality characteristics as:

*More extrovert* or *More introvert*

- More extrovert types relate more easily to the outside world of human beings and tangible objects rather than ideas.

- More introvert types relate more easily to the inner world of ideas rather than the outer world of humans and things.

*Sensing* or *Intuiting*

- Sensing types prefer to work with known facts rather than look for possibilities in relationships.

- Intuiting types prefer to look for possibilities and relationships rather than work with known facts.

*Thinking* or *Feeling*

- Thinking types base judgements more on impersonal analysis and logic than on personal values.

- Feeling types base judgements more on personal values than on impersonal analysis and logic.

*Judging* or *Perceiving*

- Judging types like a planned, decided, orderly way of life rather than a flexible, spontaneous way.

- Perceiving types like a flexible, spontaneous way of life rather than a planned, decided, orderly way.

Since the publication of Jung's *Psychological Types* (1921) much development has taken place in this field of human under-standing. Most successful persuaders seem to want to understand the mainsprings of their own behaviour and that of the people they wish to influence. If personality is such an important factor in successful human interaction, the Perfect Persuader must understand and employ basic psychology if they are to improve rapport.

The following questionnaire is a simpler and more accessible model, easy to understand and interpret. Try it on yourself (or be really daring and ask a colleague or friend to complete it on your behalf). It will tell you a lot about the way in which you influence others as well as how you yourself might prefer to be influenced.

## I do it my way

Everyone is uniquely different. Our faces are different, our bodies are different and we have differently 'shaped' personalities. There is no such thing as a right or wrong personality – they just work differently in different influencing situations.

This activity is designed to help you understand better how to influence others. The results will enable you to determine what kinds of personality you prefer to influence, as well as those personalities that may be more difficult and less comfortable for you. Whatever your personality, it will provide you with many strengths, helping you to persuade, influence and convince others. It will inevitably also reveal some blind spots in your understanding of others and the way you respond to their personalities.

## Instructions

The following questionnaire consists of 20 pairs of statements. Read each statement and circle *one* statement in *each pair* that you perceive as most characteristic of you or your behaviour in a social or work environment. Evaluate your behaviour as it is now, not as it once was or how you would like it to be.

1. A I enjoy making new friends
   B I would rather read than talk

2. C I find detail tedious and often unnecessary
   D I try to stick to the rules

3. A I love being with other people
   B I do not mind being on my own

4. C I tend to take charge
   D I am willing to be influenced by others

5. A I am comfortable talking to people I don't know
   B I am slow in developing new relationships

6. C I exert my influence on others
   D I am easy to persuade

7. A I enjoy social gatherings
   B I am just as happy to be on my own

8. C I am confident of my views and opinions
   D I am happy for others to take charge

9. A I have been accused of being 'loud'
   B I keep to a small circle of friends

10. C I express my beliefs with confidence
    D I sometimes keep quiet even when I know I am right

11. A I dislike too much detail
    B I am very thorough and careful

12. C I can plan and control the work of others
    D I am uncertain of my views

13. A I tend to be rather impulsive
    B I look before I leap

14. C I have clear aims and ambitions
    D I live each day as it comes

15. A I am an approachable person
    B I keep myself to myself

16. C I am a poor delegator
    D I seek the approval of others

17. A I make new friends easily
    B I am happy with my own company

18. C I achieve, others can look after the detail
    D I am willing to be influenced by others

19. A I am a people person
    B I take time to get to know others

20. C I take the lead in group work
    D I am easily influenced

## Scoring and interpreting the questionnaire

1. Count the number of As and Bs you circled and record the number in the spaces below. Likewise, total the Cs and Ds.

2. Subtract the number of As from the number of Bs and the Cs from the Ds.
    The differences can range from +10 to -10.

3. Transfer the difference to the scoring profile.

............ (B) minus ............ (A) = ............
............ (D) minus ............ (C) = ............

## Scoring profile

EXTROVERT                    (B minus A)                    INTROVERT
-10 -9 -8 -7 -6 -5 -4 -3 -2 -1 0 +1 +2 +3 +4 +5 +6 +7 +8 + 9 +10


DOMINANT                     (D minus C)                    SUBMISSIVE
-10 -9 -8 -7 -6 -5 -4 -3 -2 -1 0 +1 +2 +3 +4 +5 +6 +7 +8 + 9 +10


## Transferring and understanding your score

To obtain a graphic representation of the relative importance of each score to your overall behaviour, transfer your B minus A score and mark it on the horizontal axis on page 99. Now transfer your D minus C score and mark it on the vertical axis.

Unless either of your scores was a zero, you can now join up the two marks within one of the four quadrants (see example).

Your final score will reveal you to be one of four personality types:

• Dominant/Extrovert

• Submissive/Extrovert

• Dominant/Introvert

• Submissive/Introvert.

**Extreme scores:** Respondents whose scores are closest to one of the four outer corners of the main box are extreme examples. Your scores will be on the high side, between plus or minus 6 to 10.
**Average scores:** Respondents whose scores are in the range plus or minus 3 to 5 are average.
**Neutral scores:** Respondents whose scores range between 0 and plus or minus 2 are neutral.

DOMINANT

```
                          C
                        -10
                        - 9
                        - 8
                        - 7
                        - 6
                        - 5
                        - 4
                        - 3
                        - 2
                        - 1
EXTROVERT  A -10-9-8-7-6-5-4-3-2-1 1 2 3 4 5 6 7 8 9 10 B  INTROVERT
                          1
                          2
                          3
                          4
                          5
                          6
                          7
                          8
                          9
                         10
                          D
```

SUBMISSIVE

Although this model is a simplified interpretation of Jung's find-ings, most of his key personality characteristics can be overlaid on it. By recognising and interpreting the effect of these characteris-tics, you can adjust more easily to another's personality.

To engage more successfully with a wide range of individuals and stand a better chance of persuading and influencing change, you need to be prepared to amplify (or suppress) the appropriate characteristics of your own personality. To guide you through this model I have created a matrix, with each of the four personality 'types' given a name. It will help you identify the personalities of those people who you need to influence. As a by-product you may begin to realise exactly why it is that you seem to get on better with some people rather than others.

Developed as a matrix, the personality model looks like this:

DOMINANT

|  | |
|---|---|
| Proactive<br><br>LEADER | Analytical<br><br>LISTENER |
| Creative<br><br>TALKER | Reactive<br><br>FOLLOWER |

EXTROVERT · · · · · · · · · · · · · · · · · · · · INTROVERT

SUBMISSIVE

I use this model frequently in training seminars presented around the world. A question I usually ask the people present is: 'To which of the four personality types do you least like presenting your case?' The results are fascinating. Most salespeople dislike analytical listeners and reactive followers. Most accountants dislike creative talkers. Most entrepreneurs dislike reactive followers. And so on.

Research shows that two personality traits attract one another:

- Those who look after or lead (someone who is dominating) are attracted to those who want to be looked after or guided (someone who is submissive) and vice versa. This is known as nurturing and succouring.

- Some domineering people include the bullying boss (or husband or wife!) who feels more fulfilled when surrounded by sycophantic, subservient slaves. Nurturing/succouring does not enter these relationships.

If you are more submissive than dominant, this is not to say that you should change your personality. Just modify certain aspects – if necessary – when in the company of more dominant types. If you are influencing or persuading someone who dominates, it would be unwise to show yourself as being too submissive. If you doubt this, ask yourself: 'Who does a dominating person play golf with at the weekend?' A bunch of submissive people? Of course not. Most true dominant types revel in the company of other dominant people. To get alongside a dominant personality, bring out your own dominant characteristics and use your rapport and matching skills. In short, if you feel that a 'personality conflict' is interfering with your relationship, it is important to notice early on whether the other person has a role which they prefer playing and to make the necessary adjustments. If you don't adjust, it is unlikely that the person you are attempting to convince will alter.

# Personality models analysed

To help identify and understand the four 'types', here is a detailed analysis of the personality matrix. Each personality type has plus and minus points, which can help or hinder your efforts.

## Proactive leaders: want to be in charge

For a lot of people, influencing proactive leaders is an uphill struggle. This character wants to dominate every conversation in which they are involved. Most people find this quite intimidating. Every time you manage to get a word in edgeways and start to make a suggestion or two, the proactive leader ignores you or hijacks your ideas and claims them as their own. Here lies the main route to convincing a proactive leader – let them think that your ideas *are* theirs. Do not worry unnecessarily that it is your idea. The point is that they think it is theirs. Let them believe this – after all, your main objective is to gain commitment – and you have got it.

Another way through the bluster and bluff is to engage in the fight. Proactive leaders despise very submissive behaviour in those with whom they cannot engage in a juicy fight. They relish a battle and like to feel that they have 'won' a victory.

Often a self-made person (and proud of it), this character can appear coarse and materialistic. They can be egotistical and conscious of status (measured by anything from age to height, job title to wealth, size of car to membership of exclusive clubs). All possible arguments should be expressed in ways that boost their prestige and affirm their perceived status. Don't worry too much about flattery. Proactive leaders expect to be flattered – it is all part of their motivation. Use power words like 'best, biggest, unique to you, powerful, first, ahead of the pack, money, beat the competition'.

If this seems unsubtle – it is! But subtlety is not their style. Ask for their opinion, allow them to be magnanimous. Proactive leaders can be kind as well as bullies.

## Positive and negative characteristics

+ Planner; goal-setter; disciplined; organised; open to new ideas; enjoys open power; appears confident; authoritative; makes statements; task-oriented; makes quick decisions; can be kind and helpful.
- Insensitive; easily bored; bullies people; aggressive; overbearing; impatient; direct; ruthless; a poor delegator.

## Analytical listeners: want to feel in charge

Like the proactive leader, the analytical listener is dominant. They are often aloof and quiet. This type prefers you to do all the talking, hoping perhaps that you will talk your way out of your own argument or, even better, make mistakes and reveal the weaknesses of your case. Analytical listeners are objective, focused and, above all, cool. Carefully framed questions will bring them out of their shells. They like proposals to be in writing. Be prepared to provide plenty of background detail and testimonials. Use their ideas and opinions to support your case. Expect the analytical listener to take time in responding to your proposition.

Power words and phrases which will help your argument include 'statistical proof, evidence, facts and figures, research, profit, logical, reason'.

Analytical listeners are strongly independent. They genuinely want to think things over. This need should not necessarily be seen as a put-off. The classic analytical listener did not get where they are today by making hasty decisions. They want to assess all the data. Be prepared to put your case in writing so that they can go over the arguments in their own time. Provide plenty of charts, graphs and tables. Analytical listeners love poring over them. But make quite sure they are accurate. This type searches for inaccuracies and derives fiendish pleasure in discovering a few.

## Positive and negative characteristics

+ Thorough; persistent; calm; relishes hidden power; formal; disciplined; active; thoughtful; subtle; deliberate; objective; rational; analytical; logical; loves figures.
- Perfectionism slows the decision process; aloof; procrastinates; closed to new ideas; hates open persuasion; outwardly unemotional; cruel sense of humour; distant; slow to trust; bureaucratic; demands evidence.

## Reactive followers: seek a dependent relationship

Like the analytical listener, these types are also reserved people. Reactive people wait for others to take the initiative and then follow. They can appear timid and uncertain. They need to consider and analyse before acting, relying heavily on advice and counsel from a wide variety of sources. The reactive follower has a long record of bad decisions. Because of this they rarely attain a position of authority, especially one where contacts with the outside world involve purchasing or making major decisions. However, there are plenty of managers and owners of small businesses around, who epitomise the classic reactive follower type. When this is the case, their position will often have been reached by default or inheritance. The reactive follower is a most loyal employee and should on no account be pushed or manipulated.

Power words which work particularly well include 'security, safety, guaranteed, reliability, popular, tried and tested, proven'.

As decisions can take considerable time it is important to maintain the relationship. Do not leave the reactive follower to make decisions on their own. Keep by their side, helping, showing, supporting, proving. You will almost certainly have to expend considerable support effort, which can become frustrating. But if this means that you are eventually seen by the reactive follower as someone to trust and rely on, then all the time and effort you spend will turn out to be a worthwhile investment.

## Positive and negative characteristics

+ Good listener; dependable; friendly; passive; gentle; quiet; thoughtful; informal; loyal; people-oriented.
- Cautious; easily acquiesces; submissive; slow to trust; requires proof; relies on advisers; hates detail; dislikes change.

## Creative talkers: want a social relationship

More salespeople have fallen foul of this type than perhaps any other. The problem is simple. At first glance the creative talker appears such a sociable and friendly type, so helpful and supportive, making everything seem plain sailing. This is often an illusion. The creative talker's chief concern is to get people to like them. They are, above all, people persons, they want to be liked and are keen to maintain relationships with others. Their approach to business can be sloppy and disorganised. They make and break promises, miss appointments, keep you waiting.

The key to a successful dialogue with the creative talker is control. Control the conversation: 'I have called today, Mister Creative Talker, in order to discuss the MacCallum project.' This statement anchors your objective at the outset. Every time the creative talker changes the subject, you can get it back on track by 'going back to the reason for our meeting'.

Power words that work well with this type include 'fun, appreciate, enjoy, convenient, easy, trouble-free, inexpensive'.

The creative talker can be fun to be with, but beware – they are sometimes so anxious to preserve the friendship that solutions may never be found or decisions agreed.

## Positive and negative characteristics

+ Responsive; talkative; very sociable; friendly; informal; warm; approachable; creative; relishes new ideas; enthusiastic.
- Undisciplined; poor time-keeper; disorganised; impulsive; gullible; easily led; impatient; overgeneralises; gets emotional and nostalgic.

# Part two

# Tools and techniques

# 9   Styles of influence

Most people have a preferred natural way of persuading others which seems to work some of the time. But if you always do what you've always done, you'll always get what you always got. The Perfect Persuader has a whole armoury of styles and strategies, all polished and practised, tried and tested. If what you are doing is not working, do something else, anything else. In any dialogue or interaction, the person who has the greatest flexibility, the most choices of what to do, will be in control of the situation. More choices = more successes.

There are several identifiable ways and means to persuade others of the value of your ideas. Greater proficiency in a wider range of strategies will lead to greater success.

- **Empowerment:** Make others feel valued by giving them praise and encouragement.

- **Interpersonal awareness:** Identify other people's concerns and embrace them within your proposals.

- **Bargaining/negotiation:** Gain support and a win–win conclusion by offering to exchange favours or resources (*never* give concessions away – *always* trade them for something you want in return). Don't just share the cake – make it a bigger one.

- **Relationship building:** Build rapport and take the time to get to know others personally – what are their interests, values, beliefs, wants and needs?

- **Organisational awareness:** Become a brilliant networker; identify key people and get their support.

- **Common vision:** Show how your ideas support the broader goals of the organisation or group.

- **Impact management:** Present your ideas or proposals in such a graphic, dramatic or memorable way as to gain the support of others.

- **Logical persuasion:** Use logical reasons, facts, data and evidence to convince others. Be prepared to allow the other person time to respond or make up their mind.

- **Emotional persuasion:** Use emotive statements to attract agreement or compliance (this approach can border on manipulation and may carry with it some risks: it can leave a nasty taste in the mouth, and painful memories linger long).

- **Power or structural authority:** Relies on your status, rank, title or position in order to get your way. Similar to the Push/directive style (see page 111).

- **Coercion:** Use threats or pressure to get others to do what you want. Can work well if you have the power and authority to follow it through. But this approach is more likely to invoke rebellious behaviour or sullen passivity.

- **Assertion:** State your case or requirements unemotionally and repetitiously, explaining how agreement will affect you ('I find your behaviour irritating and want you to find ways to avoid it in future'). Works well with autocratic people, bullies and stick-in-the-muds. Best used as an active rather than reactive approach.

- **Push or directive style:** Clarify, explain, inform, propose, suggest, disagree, state difficulties. Used when looking for a quick response. Use of this style often results in short-term commitment so will need following through.

- **Pull or collaborative style:** Seek ideas or information, seek clarification, build on the ideas of others, agree or support. Likely to produce a slow but ultimately committed response.

- **Passive or covert style:** Influence by example or personal demonstration of desired behaviours. Can be a frustratingly lengthy journey but persistence will pay off.

## Choosing the right approach

*One judges everyone by one's own standard and from one's own standpoint.*
M. Esther Harding, psychoanalyst, 1888–1971

I have a good friend, born in February, which makes her an Aquarian. Whether you believe in astrology or not, she typifies the sign of the water carrier. She has a great need for freedom and is strong-willed with firm convictions. However, she is slightly detached and unpredictable and will not be pushed, bullied or browbeaten. If anyone tries to make her do anything against her will or better judgement, they find their pressure has the reverse effect. Once she has dug her heels in they won't easily be prised out. The autocratic approach is doomed to failure. Even a careful argument backed up with plenty of proof and statistical evidence is challenged, queried and wrestled to death before any grudging acceptance is granted. A wholly passive approach is equally fruit-less and frustrating. 'Well come on,' she'll say. 'What do you think? If you don't know the answer, you can't expect me to know what it is.' Probably a 'democratically assertive negotiation' is the only possible route to success with my exasperating friend.

Another friend is quite the reverse. He can never make up his mind. Give him two or more choices and you can wait for ever for a decision. If you try the democratic approach this only offers him even greater scope for vacillation (something his friends suspect that he rather enjoys). Providing a passive response will lead even-tually to a total communication vacuum. A good deal of the time he actually *likes* to be told what to do. If others are successfully doing it too, then he is even more convinced (he would hate to be a guinea pig for some half-baked idea that has not been thor-oughly road-tested). He wants proof and supportive evidence to shore up his eventual decision. One of his greatest fears is being held up to ridicule after he has made what he thinks is a carefully considered choice. 'Oh no, you didn't fall for that old scam surely? They must have seen you coming a mile off.'

Here are two individuals who respond quite differently to influ-ence. Behaviour which one finds unacceptable is highly produc-tive with the other. Knowing the person you are influencing should be a prerequisite for eventual success. But what if you have never met them before? Recently I was introduced to someone who worked in a senior position in a management consultancy firm. They told me their organisation was expanding and becoming increasingly involved in a wider range of assignments. I probed for further details: the type of work carried out by the consult-ants, the market sectors on which they concentrated and so on. I asked for a copy of the company's brochure with the name of the managing director.

My objective was to persuade the organisation to take me on

their books or add my details to their database as a prospective consultant for future assignments. I wrote to the senior partner outlining my background and detailed a few current clients who in some way aligned with their own field of operation. By return, I received a letter inviting me to meet the consultancy director. OK so far, the first hurdle successfully jumped. The only problem was that I had never met the director in question. What was their background? What type of personality did they have? How old were they? Did they dress formally or informally?

I asked my friend, the original contact, all these questions and more. Gradually I built up a clear picture of the person I was to meet. First I carefully reviewed my own work experience, looking for anything which might dovetail with theirs. On the morning of the meeting I considered what I would wear, taking care to choose a shirt and tie which would signal that we were on the same level, or at least not from a different planet altogether. Knowing a little more about their personality I was able to get myself into the right frame of mind before the meeting even began. I visualised the conversation; thought through my responses to anticipated questions. When we finally met, the care and thought which I had invested paid off. There was still the need to get to know one another at the start; still the need to go over my letter and curriculum vitae; but the pre-planning seemed to accelerate these formalities. Everything went faster and smoother than it often does when we meet someone for the first time.

Influencing behaviour is multifaceted. From one communication to another we need to practise behavioural flexibility, providing ourselves with the maximum opportunity for success. Each of us will be naturally and instinctively better able to deal with certain situations than others. Our strengths see us through. The only way to successfully influence change in different people and personalities is to learn and develop the widest possible range of influencing styles. Knowing your preferred styles will create a good foundation for further personal development and growth.

The following questionnaire has been designed to reveal your strengths and weaknesses as well as your preferred influencing styles.

## How do you prefer to communicate?

Depending on what outcome you want, how much commitment you seek, how important the ongoing relationship is – you will need to choose the style most suitable and follow it through. This activity will help you develop an awareness of your natural influencing styles.

## Instructions

The following questionnaire consists of 32 pairs of statements. Circle *one* statement in *each pair* which best describes your behaviour in most influencing situations, most of the time.

1.  A I don't give up when others disagree
    B I develop other people's ideas

2.  C I produce evidence to support my arguments
    D I feel strongly about the outcome

3.  E I make my views clear
    F I often regret not coming forward earlier

4.  G I explain the benefits of my proposals
    H I try to seek a satisfactory compromise

5. A I tell people exactly what I want
   B I seek facts and opinions

6. C I explain the facts
   D I use my enthusiasm to convince

7. E I am happy to fight my own corner
   F I keep my feelings to myself

8. G I enjoy convincing other people
   H I go for a win–win solution

9. A I put forward lots of new ideas
   B I am a good listener

10. C I provide statistical back-up where necessary
    D I can get upset if I fail to convince

11. E I express my beliefs with confidence
    F I am afraid to admit my ignorance

12. G I plan answers to likely objections
    H I trade concessions – give and take

13. A I contribute plenty of suggestions
    B I build on other people's ideas

14. C I construct a good logical argument
    D I feel it personally if I fail to influence

15. E I tell people clearly how I feel
    F I feel uncomfortable with compliments

16. G I push for an early decision
    H I enjoy bargaining with others

17. A I am comfortable challenging the views of others
    B I am willing to be influenced by others

18. C I put my case in writing
    D I sweep people up with my enthusiasm

19. E I believe I have the right to say 'no'
    F I feel uncomfortable in unfamiliar surroundings

20. G I can quickly think up a counter-argument
    H I see the point of view of both sides

21. A I am not afraid to suggest solutions
    B I accept criticism without becoming defensive

22. C I provide step-by-step details
    D I skip detail – I influence through my personality

23. E I express my displeasure when appropriate
    F I do favours even when I prefer not to

24. G I enjoy getting people to change their minds
    H I am concerned about maintaining the
       relationship

25. A I feel comfortable giving orders
    B I listen carefully to people who disagree with me

26. C I present my ideas in an organised way
    D I am elated when I succeed in influencing

27. E I don't mind asking for help when necessary
    F I don't like hurting others' feelings

28. G I learn all the features and benefits of my proposals
    H I try to understand the viewpoint of the other person

29. A I explain carefully my requirements
    B I am content to support other people's ideas

30. C I use facts to convince others
    D My enthusiasm is contagious

31. E I express my feelings honestly and directly
    F I try to maintain popularity with others

32. G I am not put off when others object
    H I avoid conflict and seek a happy medium

## Scoring and interpreting the questionnaire

1. Count the number of As and Bs you circled and record the number in the spaces on page 118. Likewise, total the Cs and Ds, the Es and Fs, the Gs and Hs.

2. Subtract the number of As from the number of Bs, the Cs from the Ds, the Es from the Fs and the Gs from the Hs.

The differences can range from +8 to -8. Transfer the difference to the scoring profile.

............ (B) minus ........... (A) = ...........

............ (D) minus ........... (C) = ...........

............ (F) minus ........... (E) = ...........

............ (H) minus ........... (G) = ...........

## Scoring profile

A = AUTOCRATIC                    B = DEMOCRATIC
-8 -7 -6 -5 -4 -3 -2 -1 0 +1 +2 +3 +4 +5 +6 +7 +8

C = LOGICAL                       D = EMOTIONAL
-8 -7 -6 -5 -4 -3 -2 -1 0 +1 +2 +3 +4 +5 +6 +7 +8

E = ASSERTIVE                     F = PASSIVE
-8 -7 -6 -5 -4 -3 -2 -1 0 +1 +2 +3 +4 +5 +6 +7 + 8

G = PERSUADER                     H= NEGOTIATOR
-8 -7 -6 -5 -4 -3 -2 -1 0 +1 +2 +3 +4 +5 +6 +7 +8

## Extreme scores - plus or minus 6, 7 or 8

If you scored at this level you probably tend to use that style rather than its paired opposite (for example, assertive rather than passive). This could be because:

- you work in an organisation or group where this influencing style is the cultural norm

- you work for or closely associate with an individual who expects you to use this approach (possibly they use it a lot)

- you work in a job or function where this way of influencing is recognised as appropriate

- none of the above applies – you simply prefer to behave that way.

## Balanced scores – plus or minus 2, 1 or zero

If any of your scores fell within this range it suggests that you are equally able and prepared to use both paired styles (for example, directive or collaborative). This provides you with greater flexibility of operation across a wider spectrum of influencing scenarios.

What do the scores suggest about your preferred style of persuading? What are the likely gains and losses if you continue to use your preferred style? Are these the gains you seek? If you want a different outcome, which of your preferred styles will you need to change in some way?

# Which persuasion style will work best?

There are normally three main objectives to be kept in mind whenever you influence others:

- you want to maintain an existing relationship

- you aim to gain long-term commitment to your proposal

- you wish to ensure your message is passed on to other people.

All influence produces some sort of reaction. On a scale of one to five these are the most likely reactions you will receive:

1. Total commitment: 'Brilliant idea. Can't wait to start.'

2. Broad agreement: 'Like the idea but I have one or two questions.'

3. Compliance: 'OK. If that's what you want. You're the boss.'

4. Disagreement: 'There are three good reasons why this won't work.'

5. Sabotage: 'I may have agreed to do it but I'll prove it won't work.'

## Are they *really* committed?

Recall a situation where you successfully managed to gain commitment from another person, or people. As you think back to that time when you were successful, begin to remember what it was you said or did which resulted in the commitment you sought.

What signals told you that the other person/people were committed?

- What did you see?

- What did you hear?

- What did you feel?

Will you want to repeat your success or alter your approach?

# Eight strategies used by Perfect Persuaders

## The autocratic, directive, push approach

Autocracy generally works best when it is accompanied and supported by power, authority, status, experience or age. You are the captain of the ship and what you say goes. The benefits this brings to the influencing process are few but significant. First, autocracy is a fast and efficient way of persuasion. It is unlikely there will be any serious objections to be overcome. The process will probably take the form of a monologue, rather than a dialogue. You will issue commands and encounter little or no resistance. Tell, rather than sell.

Although fast and efficient, autocracy does have its downside. Because it is a one-way street for the people on the receiving end, they have little opportunity to contribute to your proposal. It is presented as a *fait accompli* with full commitment expected. This expectation frequently backfires, especially when long-term commitment is required. The problem often stems from the other person feeling 'You won and I lost'. Effective for short-term influencing – when you gain commitment, be prepared to check and double-check your proposals are being carried out. Only use your autocratic power when a short-term change is sought. Do not be surprised if buy-in is weak. Be prepared to enforce commitment.

## The democratic, collaborative pull approach

The joy of the more democratic approach is that it works successfully without requiring to be backed up by power. You don't need to be in charge or have any formal authority or status over others. Because you have included them in the decision process, your ideas will receive high commitment. Democratic influence over others is therefore low risk and usually needs little enforcement as it is seen as 'you win/I win'. Because others contribute to and support your proposition, this style of influence is most effective for long-term influencing. You will not need to enforce the agreement – too much 'policing' by you could even result in a withdrawal of support. If you do feel the need to follow up, be sure to do it elegantly, discreetly and with empathy.

Democracy is slow and not without some risks. True democracy means handing over the entire decision process to others. They may take their time and even resent it if you chivvy and chase them for a resolution. Who is to say they will arrive at the 'answer' you seek? Suppose it is radically different and largely unworkable? Because you invited their input they are now committed, so will take a dim view if you decide to change requirements at this stage.

It is likely that you will want to think things through carefully before handing over the decision to others. Questions you may want to address could include:

- How long can I afford to wait for a decision?

- How many people can I usefully delegate this to?

- Who should I delegate it to?

What parameters should they work within? The more democratic choices you can offer, the more commitment you will receive. The fewer parameters or conditions you impose, the better. Democracy takes time – be sure to give it time.

## The logical approach

Many people favour a logical explanation before reaching a decision. They may go overboard, demanding a blow-by-blow account of the background details, how you reached your conclusions, how many conclusions you examined, why you chose your particular recommended solution. For many of us, this relentless concentration on detail can be tiresome. After all, we are anxious to get on with the matters in hand. After a while we feel that it may be better not to bother at all.

The logical approach to influence can have very positive rewards. First it makes us examine and re-examine our arguments. No amount of enthusiasm will make someone agree to our suggestions if they have a detailed, logical, linear mind. The creative, spontaneous approach does not appeal to this type. The only way we can be certain of a sympathetic ear to our argument is to do our homework. Leave nothing to chance – no guesswork, no exaggeration – just straightforward unassailable facts. And the more of them the better.

## The emotional approach

Appealing to the various emotions that swirl around within the human heart and mind can be dangerous. When emotions are captured by dubious arguments, the result can be long-held feelings of remorse and anger. No one likes to be duped, especially when it is later revealed that decisions were based on emotions rather than logic or good sense. Emotional decisions are frequently made on impulse. Perhaps feelings of sorrow or anger, love or hatred may tempt us to be pushed into a hasty decision. We have all encountered so-called emotional blackmail at some time in our lives. So whenever you attempt to harness other people's emotions take care to examine the likely outcome. If you desire a long-term commitment with no bad aftertaste or unnecessary remorse, appealing to emotions can be a very effective way of influencing. The creative talker can be particularly susceptible to an emotional appeal.

Having checked the integrity of your objectives and motives, it is quite in order to turn on the charm and enthusiasm. Persuading others to feel part of your exciting project or idea is an extension of your own feelings. Enthusiasm has been defined as 'knowledge on fire'. Use your knowledge and enthusiasm to fire up the imaginations of others. This approach works well with those who are themselves emotional or impulsive. If they become swept up in the excitement of a project, they are also likely to be captured by the charm, charisma or sheer enthusiasm of the influencer. By appealing to the long-term effects of your ideas, you will also be stressing the continuing value that will result from your ideas.

Some power words which work well could include 'pleasure, happiness, love, security, admiration, appreciation, satisfaction'.

Appealing to the emotions carries with it a risk. Check your motives carefully and remember that although this approach can be successful it can also leave a nasty taste in the mouths of those you persuade. Painful memories linger long – they'll get you next time!

## The assertive approach

Assertiveness is the use of clear and unambiguous language. By expressing your feelings, you ask directly and confidently for what you want (or do not want). Being assertive does not involve aggression – simply firmness.

Maintain good eye contact, speak in a level and pleasant tone and express your needs unequivocally and concisely.

- Making a request: 'I need you to complete the report by Friday afternoon, please.'

- Refusing a request: 'I'm sorry but I won't be able to give you a hand today. I have too much on at the moment.'

Coupled with assertiveness, persistence can work wonders. This is a technique known as 'broken record'. You make your statement and depending on the response you get, you repeat it in a slightly different form. You do this as many times as is necessary for the other person to fully understand your intent. For example:

> 'Can you get this word-processed by 12 o'clock, please?'
> *'I have to finish this report first.'*
> 'I appreciate what you say but this document must be ready for this afternoon's board meeting.'
> *'But this will only take another hour.'*
> 'It will have to be delayed in that case.'
> *'I'm sure I can get both done in time.'*
> 'That is not good enough. I need it by 12 noon. I'll leave it with you and call back in an hour to see how you are progressing.'

Assertiveness is particularly helpful when dealing with unwanted or undesirable behaviour in others. It is important to express clearly *how* the other person's behaviour is affecting you. For example:

> 'I find it offensive when you say things like that. Please stop.';
> 'Your behaviour is inappropriate. It embarrasses me and I want you to stop it right away.'

Assertive influence works effectively with autocratic people and those who least expect assertion from you. You believe in yourself, you act and initiate, rather than react.

## The passive approach

At first glance this seems an improbable notion. How can a person be passive or submissive and yet influence others and control the outcome? The passive approach suggests that the rights and needs of others take precedence over your own. If not controlled properly this can result in feelings of low self-esteem, frustration and even withdrawal.

However, suppose that another driver cuts you up and, after you shake your fist at him, he stops and approaches your car. What do you do now? He is bigger, younger and fitter than you. Any major argument could well lead to a physical encounter. You decide to let the matter rest and make a joke of it. This means that you have to swallow your pride and back off. Some might say that this was wimpish behaviour. Others would agree that you took the sensible view and cut your losses while you still had the time.

A friend was recently flagged into a lay-by by the traffic police. Clearly, he'd committed some offence but was unsure what it was. He immediately got out of his car and approached the policeman. 'Oh, dear,' he said, 'I've obviously been a naughty boy.'

Recognising that in these circumstances traffic police behave rather like critical parents, my friend decided to oblige by adopting the role of the obedient child. It worked and he was let off with a caution.

The option of influencing outcomes through submission is certainly viable as long as you can live with any feelings of regret or embarrassment it might create within you after the event.

## The sales approach

Most people run a mile when they see a salesperson on the horizon. We all have tales to tell of the archetypal pushy salesperson who pins you up against a wall and tries to thrust some product or service down your throat. Never mind whether you actually want it or not – the one they're selling is cheaper, faster, bigger and you would be a fool not to take up their unique offer. Then there's the cold call. Just when you are sitting back in your chair for the first time all day, the telephone or doorbell rings – and it's your 'friendly' salesperson reading out boring product details from a script.

There is often a case to be made for good old-fashioned salesmanship. Many people actually like to be sold to. Stroll through any street market anywhere in the world and you'll see crowds of happy punters positively lapping up the sales spiel. Recently a neighbour was cold-called by a salesman selling a carpet-cleaning product. She agreed to see him and after an hour in his company was flicking through her telephone book, willingly providing him with names and numbers of all her closest friends. She was so taken with his sheer salesmanship and youthful exuberance that it seemed almost churlish not to oblige when he asked her to 'help him reach his sales targets' by giving him some referred leads. She truly appreciated his skill.

Although most of us profess not to like the sales type, we are, after all, perpetual buyers. Hardly a day goes by when we aren't in and out of shops, or on the internet or telephone checking comparative prices. In a typical year we might make major purchasing decisions to buy a car, a holiday or even a job. And in most cases we will expect some sort of salesmanship to come into play. We are buyers – and buyers need salespeople.

The upfront 'sales' approach works well with anyone who expects to be sold to. A carefully planned sales case clearly shows how benefits match needs, objections can be overcome and going for a clear decision makes all the sense in the world. The extrovert creative talker is often more accepting of the overt sales approach. Make sure you have a watertight case if 'selling' your ideas to an analytical listener or a reactive follower.

With those who hate the overt 'sales' approach, try bridging. First, draw out the other person's point of view through careful questioning. Check their values and beliefs. Next, demonstrate through rapport skills that you understand their point of view.

Empathise without necessarily sympathising. Finally, lead them towards agreement by giving credit and praise in response to their good ideas and suggestions. Join your views with theirs and avoid cognitive dissonance. Demonstrate whenever you can exactly how your proposals dovetail with their own ideas and feelings.

## The negotiating approach

For a lot of people there is little to distinguish negotiating from selling. Frequently a sale will end in negotiations and the edges become blurred. The art of bargaining is as old as mankind's own history. Adam Smith, the 18th-century economist, suggested:

> *Man is an animal that makes bargains. No other animal does this – no dog exchanges bones with another.*

When salesperson meets potential buyer for the first time there is an imbalance. The salesperson's desire to sell something can often exceed the buyer's desire to purchase. But it may be possible to add value through creative negotiation. Not just sharing the cake but making the cake bigger. When we agree to bargain, the need to buy roughly equals the need to sell. Proposals and counter-proposals lead eventually to an agreeable solution. Given common needs, skilful negotiation can swiftly lead to an acceptable win–win resolution.

One question should be at the forefront of anyone's mind when about to embark on a negotiation:

'To what extent do I need to maintain this relationship?'

If the answer is 'very little', then it may not be necessary to conduct a fair negotiation. You can be as tough as it is possible to get away with. (This does not imply the use of underhand tactics, lying or cheating. However, the lack of an ongoing relationship between buyer and seller may result in either side agreeing to a solution that is ultimately found to be lacking in fairness. This will matter less if neither side are likely to find themselves facing each other across a negotiating table.)

Good negotiators realise the importance of the ongoing relationship and work hard to seek a win–win resolution. Flexibility allows them to trade concessions for concessions. Very little is given away. Not surprisingly, negotiation works well with anyone, such as the professional buyer, who expects to negotiate the final outcome. Here are a few basic rules:

- Set your sights high. You will inevitably have to lower them during your negotiation so it makes sense to aim high at the start. But not so high that it makes a negotiated outcome appear impossible.

- Find out what people want before you begin the negotiation. They are bound to have a package of needs and unless you take care to note (in writing) their 'shopping list' before starting the dialogue, there is every chance they will spend the whole negotiation producing one unexpected demand after another. Then when you run out of concessions to trade, you will be forced to agree to their remaining demands in order to reach a final solution.

- Don't give anything away. Always trade concessions. Give something away that they want, get something back you want. Even the most unlikely elements can be traded for one another (time concessions for cost reductions; agreeing to leave the house you are selling earlier than you would like in order to be able to take the hall light fitting with you; asking for a better-grade car in return for a lower salary increase). Take care in evaluating the worth of a concession. It is easy to say 'yes' to a request because the concession holds little value for you. Ask yourself: 'This is of importance to me – but how much is it worth to the other person?'

- Be flexible. Continue to seek even the most improbable way out of any impasse. Both sides want to negotiate a solution so there should not be any need for the discussion to founder on apparently insoluble sticking points. If things really grind to a halt, suggest a break.

# 10 Moving on from a 'no'

Think back to a time when you were close to agreeing a proposal then, for some reason, you became disillusioned with the offer and pulled out of the deal at the last minute. The chances are you did not tell the other person exactly why you had changed your mind. It may have been embarrassing to tell them. Quite often resistance to the influence of others can be an intangible 'something' that went wrong. It need not relate to the nature of the offer. It may not be the costs involved. Not even the time frame. It could be something as simple as 'service', or lack of it.

## Why people resist the influence of others

Take this example. A friend of mine, Steve, was keen to buy his wife a second-hand car. During his lunch breaks he spent some time doing the rounds of car showrooms. Eventually he found exactly the car he was looking for – a one-owner Volkswagen with sunroof, radio and in a colour they both liked. At the weekend he took the money out of his bank and went with Meg to the showroom. After ten minutes they both left – without the car! Why did this happen? The car was the right one, the money was available,

Meg wanted a car. What was it that got in between their real needs and their willingness to make a decision to buy? Something took place that put them off buying. It was the service they received (or complete lack of service).

They walked into the showroom, keen and eager to go ahead, but there was no one in sight. They waited around for five minutes, but still no salesperson. When one finally arrived, they could not trace any record of Steve's earlier visit or find the documents he had completed. 'Can you come back a bit later? The manager's out to lunch and should be back at 2.30.' They did buy a car the following week but it was not a Volkswagen nor was it from that dealer. Probably the motor dealer had no idea why the car remained unsold – why Steve's excitement of Friday turned sour on Saturday.

Whenever someone tries to influence us we are forced to make decisions. When we do this we go on a mental journey. This can take just few a seconds or it might take hours, days or weeks to complete. However long the journey, the outcome will always be a decision to go ahead or not.

## The journey to 'yes'

The journey to 'yes' is one we all take when we make decisions and follows a path which has seven clearly identifiable signposts along the way.

*Step one: Interest*
Our interest in an idea or proposition must be caught and maintained from the start. Interest can range from passing a shop window and spotting an item which catches our eye, reading the headline in an advertisement, hearing a friend talk enthusiastically

about a recent experience, or becoming aware of new trends or fashions. Whatever it is, something or someone must grab our attention and hold it long enough for us to feel the need to move on to:

*Step two: Needs and wants*
Now our attention has been attracted, we start to ask ourselves a number of questions. Do I want this? How will I benefit? When we have satisfied ourselves (or deluded ourselves?) that we need or want what's on offer, we ask ourselves more detailed questions and move on to:

*Step three: Finding out*
This is the critical stage when we check that the idea being suggested will fulfil certain criteria. These may include outlay, value for money, size, colour, quality, length of life, serviceability and so on. Also we may consider at this stage how other people will react. If we go ahead what effect will that decision have on others? When we have received appropriate answers to the majority of these questions we move on to:

*Step four: Desire*
You have convinced yourself that you need it, it fits all your criteria – and now you want it. You have to have it. Even this is not the final step.

*Step five: Weighing it up*
It is here that you attempt an objective analysis of the ultimate value of the idea or proposal. You weigh up and balance your desire against the costs to reach a measure of the value for money this idea will bring. You may decide to re-examine alternative proposals or solutions before committing. For many this can be

crunch time, if costs outweigh desire and make the proposal attractive but impossible.

*Step six: Saying 'yes'*
Even at this stage we do not always say 'yes' immediately. Perhaps
we have to consult others before we can consult others before we can commit to the proposal.
Possibly there are implementation plans which need to be drawn
up and agreed. Some people want just one more night to sleep on it.

*Step seven: Yes! I made a really good decision*
So important, step seven. The need to verify our decision or to
reassure ourselves is very powerful. A colleague told me recently
that they had bought their partner a rug in a souk in Istanbul.
After much noisy haggling, my colleague was satisfied with the
deal and bought the rug. Or so they thought. Down the road my
colleague spotted a shop selling identical rugs and some unknown
demon urged them to 'just pop in to check that the deal was worthwhile'. It was; and they went back to their hotel satisfied. Duped
or not, they felt comfortable with the decision made.

When we are under pressure to make decisions, many thoughts
rush through our heads. Do I trust and believe the influencer? Do
I need to change? Am I happy with the way things are? Why do I
have to make my mind up right now? The proposition sounds fine
now – but how will it stand up to scrutiny in six months, a year?
And anyway I am not convinced I can afford it.

Many decisions that we make in life activate these automatic
defence mechanisms. Sometimes our early responses are just
holding strategies slipped in to give us time to think things through.
There are people who never make hasty decisions and there are
others who hate to make any decision to change. People avoid
making decisions for a variety of reasons. They may be afraid of

the outcome or what their friends and colleagues will say about their judgement. They may simply be too embarrassed to tell you why they cannot say 'yes' to your idea.

## Words that put people off

There are certain words or phrases that can create almost instant resistance in other people. Words, their context and the way in which they are evaluated is a highly subjective area which remains under study by the world's psychologists. For our purposes, let's examine a number of words and phrases which will universally create resistance in those we are attempting to persuade. Perfect Persuader Benjamin Franklin (1706–90) had a useful strategy for telling people what he thought while still maintaining rapport with them:

> *I develop the habit of expressing myself in terms of modest diffidence, never using when I advanced anything that may possibly be disputed the words 'certainly', 'undoubtedly' or any others that give the air of positiveness to an opinion, but rather say I conceive or apprehend a thing to be so and so: 'It appears to me' or 'I should not think it so or so for such and such reasons'; or 'I imagine it to be so' or 'It is so, if I am not much mistaken'.*
>
> *This habit I believe has been of great advantage to me when I have had occasion to inculcate my opinion and persuade men into measures that I have been from time to time engaged in promoting.*

Interactions between people seem to be at their most effective when emotions are positive – faster, easier, more enjoyable. When influencing others your constant goal should be always to avoid generating negative emotional responses – the ones you are trying to develop are either positive or at least neutral.

Here are other words that are almost guaranteed to produce a negative response:

- *But.* 'I agree with you entirely, but . . . ' What does this mean? You are saying: 'I do *not* agree with you entirely.' Exactly the opposite of the words used. The word 'but' is arguably one of the most destructive words in English. Its use immediately reverses the main message and creates instantaneous resistance in the listener. In future try substituting 'and' every time you feel the urge to use 'but'. In the above example your words would now read: 'I agree with you entirely *and* there is another thing I agree with . . . '

- *I disagree.* And well you might – but why tell people you disagree when you can so easily soften the blow by saying: 'I can see your point of view and I think there may be an even more effective way of . . . '

- *I assume.* Don't assume anything. Even if you assume correctly, there are people who will totally disagree with your assumptions just for the sheer hell of it. Try something softer: 'If I am right in thinking that . . . ' This leaves open the possibility that your 'assumption' could be incorrect and offers people the option to correct you. But they very rarely do if you soften the phrase.

## How to sound *really* negative

Apart from simple words like 'but' and 'if' there exist whole phrases which can have a very negative meaning to a listener:

- there are a few disadvantages

- there is only a small work-volume increase

- I cannot pretend that there won't be a few delays

- I hope you're not too busy to see me

- it isn't going to cost a fortune

- the meeting wasn't a complete waste of time

- with respect

- I hear what you say

- feel free to say 'no'

- I don't know how to put this

- I bet you're going to think.

Who owns the decision in placing value on these statements – the deliverer (you) or the receiver? How can you improve these statements and be sure that the message you have decided to give is the one that is received?

## Tell me more

Often, resistance to ideas or proposals is the result of insufficient information. Quite often, as others are talking, we only hear a portion of what they are saying. This is not necessarily a result of not listening. It is frequently because we have allowed ourselves to become distracted. Take this dialogue for example:

Influencer: I think you will find that the new system will work particularly well for people who have just started with the company. Also, how many times have you asked yourself: 'What will it cost us in lost time and lost orders if we do not update the system?' So, what do you think? Shall we go ahead?

You: I think we ought to give it time. I have got rather a lot on my plate at the moment, so come back and tell me again when the current recruitment campaign is completed. Perhaps in three months, which will give me time to complete the induction training course.

In the 50 or so words that the influencer uttered was the phrase 'people who have just started with the company'. Unknown to the influencer, this phrase was all you heard. It rang loud bells for you as you are preoccupied with the current recruitment drive. All kinds of images poured into your head: advertisements which need to be booked, media selected, who would be available to help you interview and so on. Meanwhile, the influencer is convinced that you heard the key words 'what will it cost us in lost time and lost orders?'

## You can't convince me: my mind's made up

Some people resist influence from the outset. Nobody, nowhere, nohow is going to influence them to change. So there! They start and finish the process with a closed mind. There could be a number of reasons for this.

- They don't like the influencer (poor rapport skills).

- They have already sampled the idea and it failed.

- They know someone else who tried this and had a bad experience.

- They have already incorporated something similar into their system.

- They don't see a need for what you are suggesting.

In the following dialogue between you and the influencer, other forces may be at work. Forces which also prevent a decision being made.

Influencer: I am sure you'll agree that what I'm suggesting will save you time and money. So, shall we go ahead?
You: Hmm. I think I'd rather wait a while. Maybe you could come back to me in a couple of months.

In this case you are simply unconvinced that the proposal will save time or money. You do not need more time to think it through – you need more convincing.

## Getting in first: anticipating objections and resistance

Imagine for a moment that you are a jockey; a good rider with years of experience. Today, you are entered in a brand new race on an unfamiliar course. Having arrived later than expected, you find you have no time to 'walk the course' and see for yourself the bends and jumps that lie ahead. You mount your horse, grasp the reins and the starting gate flies up. It's a straightforward race, like most others – normal bends, good going, no real competition. You are ahead by about three lengths; keep this up and the prize is yours. You approach the fences – only half a dozen, the usual thing. Over the first three without even noticing them – now for the fourth. Your horse slows his approach, half turns from the jump, then makes an attempt. Feet graze the top, a stumbled landing and you are thrown. Your race is over. You stand at the edge of the course watching the other jockeys sweep by. Objections are the 'fences' you will certainly encounter during your race to influence people. If you are ready for them you will be able easily to overcome these hurdles and you will achieve your goal. However, if you fail to handle even one objection, major or minor, you will also fail to influence other people. It is as simple as that.

## Step into their shoes

Before beginning to influence anyone, put yourself in their shoes. Empathise: imagine what you would think about the proposal if it was being made to you. What doubts, fears, misgivings or objections would you have? Perhaps you might have concerns about the financing of the proposal? What about the timing – would you be ready to decide to go ahead on the spot, or would you want to think it over? Would anyone else be involved in the decision process? Your boss, partner, financial adviser? Would other options be available to you? Would you want to take time to look at these before you make your decision? Perhaps you feel happy with the present position and don't see the need for a change?

By empathising, putting yourself in the other person's shoes, you will be able to see most objections long before they arise – and you'll have your answer ready. It may even be possible to answer the objection before it arises:

You: Chris, I realise you're concerned about the bottom line and, yes, my solution does seem a bit expensive at first glance. However, I can reassure you . . .

However, I would suggest you ask yourself this question: 'In anticipating the objection, raising it myself and then answering it, will I create unnecessary doubts or fears in the mind of the person I am trying to influence?' Sometimes it is better to let sleeping dogs lie; if you don't acknowledge the problem, it may never be raised. Either way, you must decide how you will deal with anticipated objections and walk the course before you construct your argument and enter the race.

# Be prepared to answer objections: the three key rules

There are very few areas in our lives where planning fails to pay. Treat planning as an investment. Many people are impulsive and do not plan ahead – never mind if they encounter problems, these can always be dealt with as they arise. Care and thought invested early on will invariably pay dividends in the long term. Here are three simple rules – if you follow these you need never worry again about what you should do if the other person says 'no' to your proposals.

## Have an answer to the objection

I was once accompanying a salesperson, Sam, on sales calls to see what areas of training may be needed. To start with, Sam did quite well. Then, right towards the end of the conversation, the buyer made a simple statement: 'We are very happy with our present supplier.' There was a long silence. Sam looked at the ground, then the ceiling

– finally at me! Then followed a long and rambling reply, which the buyer didn't accept, and a few minutes later we left. As we got back into the car, Sam turned to me and said: 'I knew the buyer was going to come out with that one – I just knew it.' I bit my tongue and said nothing. It had not been a good morning and to utter my thoughts at that point would not have helped matters. I wanted to scream: 'For heaven's sake, Sam! How can you go into that office *knowing* what was likely to be said . . . and not have an answer ready?'

Always have a polished response to any and every objection you think may come up. Rehearse it, remember it, try it out on a friend and get feedback from them. Did your reply make sense and was it consistent?

## Keep your answer brief

How do *you* feel about people who give you long, rambling answers to your concerns and queries? Most people feel bored and frustrated. Some even feel they are being duped. Give just the right amount of information needed to respond to the objection – no more, no less. Avoid repeating your points. Write down answers to any objections you anticipate. This will help to clarify your thinking. Put the written answer to one side for a while; on reviewing it you will find that you can edit it and make an even shorter and crisper answer.

## Get agreement that the objection has been answered

Perfect Persuaders do this all the time. Just because *you* think you have dealt with an objection, it doesn't mean that the other person thinks so too. Doubts may still linger in their mind; they may have misunderstood your answer. Ask the following question outright: 'Have I answered your question/solved the problem/convinced you, or would you like more information?' An alternative question might be: 'Before we continue, are you satisfied I have answered that point you raised?' By asking this direct question you force the other person to agree, or disagree, at a crucial point in the dialogue. If you don't ask this question how will you know for certain that you have answered their objection? How can you be sure that it won't arise again, perhaps at the end of the conversation grouped neatly under the umbrella statement: 'I'd like to think it over, there are still a few points I want to consider.'

## How to recognise the different types of objection

Although we talk loosely about people resisting our proposals, to getting an 'objection' that we couldn't answer, there is no such thing as '*an* objection'. When people resist a proposition, they usually outline one of four different types of objection.

### A condition

A condition is a watertight, copper-bottomed reason why the other person cannot under any circumstances agree to do what you are asking them. There is no way round a condition. The three main conditions you are likely to encounter are:

- I already have what you are suggesting. I am not aware of any need.

- I cannot make the decision on my own (although good planning should have revealed this a lot earlier).

- It is against company policy/the rules/the law.

Notice that the objections 'I do not have any money'; 'It is the wrong time'; and 'I want to think it over' are not included in the list of conditions. All of these standard objections can be countered with practice.

When you hear a condition and are *absolutely certain* that it is a condition, back off. Stop trying to influence, don't push any harder. It is more productive at this stage to go away and rethink your proposal; there may be a way around the problem. Talk to other people, hear their views and experiences and try again later. Don't force your views on people when they clearly can't make a decision. Sometimes it takes more courage to back out of a losing situation than it does to battle on without success. Accept the situation with serenity. As theologian Reinhold Niebuhr (1892–1971) said:

> *Give us the grace to accept with serenity what cannot be changed, the courage to change the things that should be changed, and the wisdom to distinguish the one from the other.*

## A misunderstanding

Often people will object to a proposal because they misunderstand some aspect. It could be that circumstances have altered since they first heard about your ideas. Perhaps you have altered your proposition to include features that were not previously there. The misunderstanding is easy to recognise and simple to resolve.

Them: I can't possibly make a decision today. I need time to think over what you're saying.
You: That isn't a problem. Please take your time – the project doesn't start for another six weeks, so you have plenty of time.

Meanwhile this will allow us the opportunity to study more closely how it will affect production control.

The other person thinks they are objecting; you recognise it as a misunderstanding – you clear it up. Simple, isn't it?

## Excuses, put-offs and stalling tactics

For most of us these can be among the most difficult of objections to deal with because they are also the hardest to identify. How can you tell whether a person really means:

> 'I can't afford it.'
> 'I have to talk to my partner.'
> 'It's the wrong time of year.'

These could all be genuine – but equally they could all be excuses.

The following dialogue is typical of one where the other person is desperately seeking an excuse – for whatever reason, they just don't feel able or ready to say 'no'. Notice the giveaway signals that suggest that these might be excuses.

You: OK. We've taken a fresh look at the costings – why don't we go for the 17th as a start date?
Them: Er . . . No, that's no good. I'm a bit tied up that week.
You: No problem, how about the week commencing the 21st?
Them: Ah . . . I'm on holiday that week.
You: That's OK. Your assistant Jo will be around. Together we can start to install the system while you're away.
Them: Yes, but Jo's not too familiar with the details . . .
You: In that case we could get Chris, the systems manager, to help.

Them: Um . . . I don't really want Chris to be involved at this stage . . .

And so on and so on and so on. Every time you come up with what seems to be a perfectly acceptable solution to the problems they raise, it is immediately countered with an apparently equally logical argument. Did you spot those giveaway signals?

- Liberal use of 'ers', 'ums', and 'ahs'.

- A different 'reason' was given each time you thought you had solved the problem.

- Their use of the phrase 'Yes, but . . . '

There is one simple reason why you are hearing excuses rather than logical objections: the other person is unconvinced. This is serious. If you are successfully to influence others, to gain their commitment, then conviction is of paramount importance.

What are the reasons why they may remain unconvinced?

1. They do not see a need for what you are suggesting.

2. You have not bothered to establish their needs.

3. They do see they have a need but remain unconvinced of the benefits you have outlined.

4. They do not see how they might gain from the benefits you have described.

5. You have misinterpreted their needs and are talking about the wrong benefits.

6. You have not developed sufficient rapport or empathy.

7. You are coming across as a pushy sales type.

8. They do not believe what you say.

9. They are naturally cautious and always look hard before they leap.

10. They never had any intention of accepting your suggestions.

Each of these reasons is potentially serious. It may be a case of 'back to the drawing board', to reappraise your original strategy. Talk to others about your problem. Perhaps they have experienced similar problems with this person and can throw light on your difficulties. Devise a suitable role-play scenario which accurately reflects the issues *and run the role play with you playing the part of the person to be convinced.* This can prove invaluable as you are likely to experience some of the feelings they are experiencing. This is empathy – putting yourself in someone else's position.

## Dealing with genuine objections to your idea or proposal

If the objections you are hearing are not conditions, misunderstandings or excuses – then they are almost certainly genuine. Real objections or resistances are easier to overcome because they spring from a basis of reality, or from the heart.

Sometimes we object because we seek more information or reassurance. How often have you left a shop having bought a product or service which you thought was rather costly. At the pit of your stomach lies a knot of guilt or self-doubt. 'Should I have bought this? Can I justify it? What will my partner/friend/colleague say?' This feeling of 'buyer's remorse' is common and simply means that the sales assistant failed to outweigh cost concerns with appropriate benefits.

So when someone says, 'I think it costs too much', this may well be a plea for more information, more benefit statements which will help the other person draw up their own checklist of reasons to use when they in turn are asked: 'Why did you say yes to the idea?'

Here are some typical objections along with classic responses. However, beware. Classic textbook responses are all very well but can swiftly lose their currency. As more people use them, more hear them – and they wear a bit thin after a while. So as you read and learn the classic replies, begin to be aware of how you will adjust these to suit you and the circumstances when you will start successfully to use them.

## Cost

Ask any professional salesperson: 'What is the objection you hear most? and they'll reply: cost/money/budget/too expensive/too cheap/no terms available and so on.

Here are some approaches you could take. A mathematical approach provides a simple and useful framework or mnemonic device on which to base your responses: + - x ÷

- **The plus objection:** 'Your idea is *more expensive* than the existing method.'

  Answer: 'Yes, it is more expensive at first glance, however you do gain *additional* benefits . . . ' (The plus approach highlights the extras *gained.*)

- **The minus objection:** 'The existing method is *less expensive* than your proposal.'

Answer: 'Yes, you are right it is *cheaper*, however it *does not provide* the following benefits . . . ' (The minus approach spotlights any benefits they may forgo.)

- **The multiply objection:** 'Wow! That's a lot more than I expected.'

  Answer: 'Yes, it does seem quite pricey. But remember that we are a *quality* company and you would expect to pay a little extra for our reputation and experience.' (The multiply approach reminds them of hidden or intangible extras such as quality or reputation.)

- **The divide objection:** 'That's quite a bit more than I thought it would come to.'

You: How much were you thinking of paying?
Them: Oh, about £4,000.
You: So as your investment in my idea will come to around £4,250 what you are concerned about is the additional £250, is that right?
Them: Yes.
You: Well, that shouldn't present too much of a problem. The expected life will be well over five years. But if we spread that difference over just five years, what are we talking about? Only £50 a year. The cost of a few litres of petrol.

The divide approach reduces the difference between expected expenditure and actual down to the lowest common denominator. Then, for good measure, this already much reduced figure is compared to a typical everyday outgoing such as petrol, beer, cigarettes or even bread.

## Time

No time, too much time, wrong time. However it is expressed, time is often cited as a 'reason' for not making a decision.

**Objection:** It is too early.

You: When will be a more appropriate time to go ahead?

Them: Oh, not for another couple of months.

You: (*Reframing*) That's fine. The delay will give us an opportunity to double-check things and give you greater peace of mind.

**Objection:** It is too late. We already made the decision to change last week.

You: (*Reframing*) I am sorry we missed the boat this time around but it is encouraging to hear that you do review these things from time to time. When do you think will be the next time to review?

Them: Probably in about a year.

You: (*Reframing*) Then we can use the time usefully by refining the idea even more to dovetail with your needs. Tell me – when do you think this will come up for review?

Them: Not sure.

You: (*PowerQuestion*) I understand. But if you did have an idea when it will come up for review when do you think that might be?

Whatever time or date they give you *make sure you submit your proposals before the deadline*. If you don't, you can be sure someone else will!

# Force field analysis: how to alter the status quo

Influencing for change means shifting the status quo. Quite often there is an unusual or innovative solution lurking somewhere – if only people would agree to do something about it! There are frequently problem situations in organisations, departments, clubs, families that, if nothing is done to bring about change, remain permanent fixtures as problems. This is because the problem can be viewed as a balance of forces that are working in opposite directions. You have identified the problem and have thought of plenty of reasons why it is necessary to promote change (the *driving forces* necessary to resolve the problem). Unfortunately there are very often forces of equal strength that may inhibit change (*restraining forces*).

A 'force field' consists of these two categories of force – the drivers versus the restrainers. If an analysis reveals that there are more restrainers than drivers, then the status quo is likely to remain. But change this balance in favour of more (or more convincing) drivers and you are on the road to change and success. However, an increase in the driving forces is apt to bring about an increase in the restraining forces. Permanent change requires the *removal* of all the significant restrainers.

Force field analysis is just one of the many approaches to persuasive problem-solving. It lends itself particularly well to the process of influencing for change as it encourages both sides to analyse whether it is logical or desirable to allow things to stay the same. For you, the influencer, it is vital to be armed with as many drivers for change as you can muster. You can be certain that others will have a rich selection of restrainers to counterbalance your arguments.

## How to construct a force field analysis

1. Write the target or desired state in a box in the centre of the page and draw a line from this box down the middle of the page.

```
┌ ─ ─ ─ ─ ─ ─ ─ ─ ─ ─ ─ ─ ─ ─ ─ ┐
      Reduced staff turnover
└ ─ ─ ─ ─ ─ ─ ─ ─ ─ ─ ─ ─ ─ ─ ─ ┘
```

2. Brainstorm the potential drivers. This is a particularly fruitful way of accumulating a devastating list to shore up your case. When you brainstorm drivers:

- enlist the help of a handful of creative friends

- go for quantity rather than quality

- refrain from judging or evaluating at this stage

- don't forget to brainstorm the restrainers – be fully aware of the other side's arguments.

On the left-hand side list the drivers and draw arrows up to the line for each driving force.

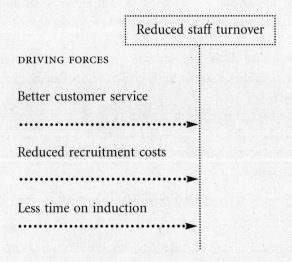

Reduced staff turnover

DRIVING FORCES

Better customer service

Reduced recruitment costs

Less time on induction

3. On the right-hand side list the restraining forces and draw arrows up to the line.

Reduced staff turnover

DRIVING FORCES                          RESTRAINING FORCES

Better customer service                 More supervision required

Reduced recruitment costs               Increased average pay rates

Less time on induction                  Planned career structure

The length of the arrows can be used to indicate stronger and weaker forces. For example, the longer the arrow, the stronger the force.

Now that you have a tighter grasp of the forces opposing change (or problem-resolution), move on to stage two of force field analysis – implementation:

- Strengthen the drivers, weaken the restrainers (brainstorm further reasons why the drivers support your case/the restrainers are weak arguments).

- Select drivers or restrainers which will be the easiest to change with the greatest pay-off.

- Devise an action plan and a strategy for influencing change through force fielding.

- Will your strategy help you achieve your objective?

- If not, which drivers or restrainers will?

There are many problem areas on which we can successfully bring our individual influence to bear. Assuming the solution will be reached automatically, or by others who have greater knowledge or superior status, can be a big mistake. How often have you seen a new system installed which was later modified, sometimes quite radically? When you talk to the people whose job it is to operate the new system they say things like: 'We knew it wouldn't work from the start.' You enquire, reasonably: 'So why didn't you say something?' They respond: 'Because nobody asked us, that's why!'

## Example: force field analysis

Suppose you are anxious to influence the outcome of a community meeting. A number of local residents are meeting to discuss the pros and cons of asking the local authority to bring in a residents' parking scheme. At present, valuable street parking spots are being taken early in the morning by people who then walk into the town centre for their work. Very often they do not return until late afternoon. This makes it difficult if not impossible for local residents to park anywhere close to home. In turn, this is awkward if you have to unload from your car or if you have small children.

You recognise that about half of those present at this evening's meeting will be against any residents' parking scheme as it will cost them money and they feel that urban parking should always be free.

Brainstorm all the drivers you can come up with – anything which will serve to back your argument. Concentrate on three or four powerful drivers and think of ways in which you might add further value to their power in the forthcoming argument.

Now do the same with the restrainers (you already have one: 'It will cost us money.'). Which restrainers are the most powerful? How can you weaken them?

Can you lessen their impact by using one or more of your drivers as a counter-argument?

We have already seen that it is necessary to gain other people's commitment to change if the outcome is not to be sabotaged or weakened. Although force field analysis is only one of many ways of tackling a problem, there are many areas where it could be useful to you, the influencer. Some examples:

- systems problems

- company policy issues

- improvements to customer service

- recruitment and selection issues

- personal or family problems

- changes of direction in life or career.

## Reframing

You glance out of the window and notice that it is raining. How typical! You have the day off – and it rains. This always seems to happen to you. You make detailed plans and they fall apart – all because of the weather. Huh!

See how easy it is to allow ourselves to enter into a downward spiral which results in feelings of disempowerment. Does this need to happen? First, we tend to blame our feelings on the weather. 'I'd be a lot happier if the sun was shining.' In fact we are *allowing ourselves to feel this way* because of some outside event. It is not the event itself which causes feelings.

Second, there are many ways of looking at things. Events can mean quite different things to different people. Question: Who will feel positively delighted that it is raining? Farmers, water authorities, fishermen, gardeners.

When you attempt to influence others they will often use some negative-sounding event as an excuse or apparent reason for not agreeing with you: 'We can't go ahead with the new software because I have three new people starting on Monday.'

How could you restate (or reframe) this statement in order to show its positive side? How about: 'That could actually be a good time to install. The three new people won't get used to the old system only to find it suddenly replaced.'

## Reframing negative words

Some people don't need a whole phrase or sentence to help enhance their feelings of helplessness. Many of us get by with just a word here and there. All of the following words slip easily into this category: angry, anxious, disappointed, embarrassed, fearful, hurt, insulted, overwhelmed, rejected, scared, stressed, terrible.

Let's take them one by one and reframe them to provide a more positive or resourceful outlook on life:

- angry = disenchanted

- anxious = a little concerned

- disappointed = surprised

- embarrassed = stimulated

- fearful = curious

- hurt = bothered

- insulted = misunderstood

- overwhelmed = challenged

- rejected = overlooked

- scared = excited

- stressed = energised

- terrible = unusual

Now reframe these typical negative power words: difficulties, dissatisfaction, worry, fear, concern, problems, doubt, won't, can't, loss.

You may be thinking that taken out of context some of these one-word reframes may sound a little insubstantial. But put them in a real-life scenario, use them and notice the difference they can make to an otherwise unproductive conversation.

## Reframing criteria: changing people's point of view

When you are asking people to make a decision you are also asking them to measure your proposition against their criteria for deciding. Criteria can be divided into:

- Tangible: cost; volume; quantity; time.

- Intangible: better-looking; more user-friendly; up-to-date; feels right.

Logical or emotional, tangible or intangible – other people's criteria are hard to argue against. But it is possible, through reframing, to change their definition by asking the question: 'What else could this mean?'

For example: 'I can't decide right now. I'll have to wait two months for the new budget to come on-stream.' This can be reframed by responding: 'Great. That two-month period will give us plenty of time to dry-run the system and ensure it is entirely free of bugs.'

To reframe apparently negative criteria ask yourself: 'What else could this mean?'

Here are some negative statements and words you may encounter. Write a statement or word for each which you feel could reframe the original in a more positive light:

- frustrated

- it's the wrong colour

- I can't afford it
- it will take too long
- insecure
- furious
- cheaper.

# 11 Reaching a decision

*With too much knowledge for the sceptic side,*
*With too much weakness for the stoic's pride,*
*He hangs between; in doubt to act or rest,*
Alexander Pope, poet, 1688–1744

People often hover on the brink of a decision, needing a gentle nudge to help them take that final step. The phrase 'influencing for change' implies a shift from one position to another, from 'no' to 'yes', from 'yes' to 'no', from inactivity to activity – a measurable departure from the status quo. In whatever way you define the change you seek, results will usually be tangible or measurable. And unless the person you are influencing offers an unconditional 'yes' to your proposals, you will need to do or say something that is intended to generate a positive decision.

This moment, the moment of deciding, is one of the most critical in the influencing process. For many people it is an anathema to have to ask: 'Shall we go ahead, then?' Why is this so often the case? There are several reasons why you may be reluctant to push for a decision, some of which are quite understandable – others less so.

# Why we are scared to ask for a decision

- Psychological reasons: consciously or unconsciously you may feel this is somehow demeaning, intrusive, manipulative, unethical or deceptive. Surely, you say to yourself, surely if the other person wants to proceed they will say so in their own good time.

- Structural authority: your own position within the organisation may be quite low down the pecking order, creating a real or perceived deterrent from asking for a decision.

- Sapiential or expert authority: the person you are influencing may not necessarily possess any real authority other than being regarded as having knowledge, expertise or wisdom. Your perception of the other person 'knowing more than I do' may cause a further weakening of intent on your part.

- Moral authority: the person you are influencing conducts themselves in such a moral, just or virtuous fashion that you feel that any pressure from you might be regarded as unseemly or distasteful.

- Dynastic authority: the Godfather Syndrome. The other person may be held in such awe by others within the family or group that it is socially unacceptable or simply not done to be seen to put any kind of pressure on them.

# Why people delay making a decision

Imagine you are reading a newspaper. Suddenly your eye is caught by an advertisement – an illustration or the promise contained in the headline has intrigued you sufficiently to stop reading a news item. You turn to the advertisement. You read it and perhaps read it again, just to be certain. Yes, you think, it sounds promising. I must do something about this. At that moment the phone rings and you put your newspaper down. Later, you pick up the paper. 'Now, where was I?' you say, turning to another news item. All positive thoughts you may have had about responding to the advertisement have evaporated. Later, you might wonder vaguely where it was you saw that advertisement but the moment has passed and despite your good intentions you never reach the final decision to do something about what you read. (This is why so many advertisements include phrases like: hurry while stocks last; rush me your catalogue; offer closes end of May. Or why there is a coupon in the bottom corner of the advertisement with a broken line around it and a drawing of a pair of scissors, just in case you are a complete idiot and are unfamiliar with how to respond!) *The road to Hell is paved with good intentions.*

Here are some reasons why people may consider putting off the evil moment of decision:

1. They do not have sufficient faith in you, your organisation/department/social group.

2. They do not fully understand the implications of your proposal.

3. They do not see how they will benefit from the ideas you put forward.

4. There are other possible options open to them.

5. Lethargy: they are content with the status quo – thank you very much.

In short – they are unconvinced.

## 'I'd like to think it over'

'I would like to give your proposals a bit of thought before I decide what to do.' This is the classic stalling tactic. We have all encountered it at some time in our lives and said it to others. But what do those words 'I'd like to think it over' suggest? Clearly the other person is still unconvinced or they would probably say 'yes' without too much hesitation.

There is a right way and a wrong way of dealing with 'I want to think about it.' Let's examine the wrong way. It is tempting to ask simply and straightforwardly: 'Why do you need to think it over?' Or perhaps: 'What is it you want to think about?'

By all means ask these questions but when you do, notice how they will almost certainly produce a response like: 'Oh, nothing really. I just didn't get where I am today by making hasty decisions.' Or, 'I always believe it helps to sleep on things.' Where does that get you? Absolutely nowhere. You are back where you started and none the wiser.

What do you need to know before you can deal with this indecision? You need to know specifically *what it is that is preventing them* from making a decision.

Now for the right way. Whenever anyone says, 'I want to think about it,' the dialogue might go something like this:

'I agree it is a difficult decision' (empathising) 'but obviously there is something you don't understand or are unhappy about . . . ' (do not pause here) ' . . . is it the time frame?'

'No, I am quite happy with that.'

'Well, is it perhaps the funding?'

'No, not really. I am confident that we can fund it through the production budget.'

'So is it the proposed project team?'

'Yes – I am not happy with Chris Parsons' involvement. We used that team on the new accounts system and found them to be very slow.'

'Is Chris's involvement the only thing which prevents you from making a decision?'

'Yes, I think everything else is fine.'

'So if I can guarantee that we won't use this team, you'd be happy to go ahead?'

'Yes.'

## How do you make decisions?

Whenever someone tries to influence us, the most critical question is: Will we say 'yes' to their proposition? This questionnaire will help you understand what influences your decisions and can throw light on the ways in which others like to make their decisions.

Read each question then circle the most appropriate answers.

A. When you choose a new car, which factors are most important to you?

1. The price
2. The dealer's reputation
3. Plenty of extras
4. The location of the dealer
5. Reliable make of car

6. Overall size of car
7. The design
8. Popular model
9. Long-term warranty available
10. Helpful staff

B. When you pick a restaurant, which of these influences your choice?

1. The basic cost of a meal
2. How well-known the chef is
3. Plenty of variety on the menu
4. How far away the restaurant is
5. Dependable food
6. How big the restaurant is
7. Its decor
8. Fashionable
9. Satisfaction assured
10. Cheerful waiting staff

C. If you were to join a new company, which factors would influence you the most?

1. The salary
2. Its reputation in its field
3. Offers varied career paths
4. How close to home is it
5. Quality of goods/ services made
6. The size of the organisation
7. How modern the office/factory shop is
8. A nationally/ internationally known company
9. A contract of employment
10. A good crowd to work with

D. When selecting a holiday hotel, which factors would you consider the most important?

1. The cost per night
2. The reputation of the hotel
3. Plenty of things to do and see
4. How long the journey will take
5. How many stars the hotel has

6. Large/medium/small hotel
7. Attractive design
8. Famous place to stay
9. Agent is a member of ABTA
10. Efficient and helpful hotel staff

E. If you were choosing a house, what would influence you the most?

1. Its price
2. District has a good reputation
3. Its potential for development
4. Its distance from facilities
5. Well-built property
6. How many rooms it has
7. Its interior design
8. It is a fashionable area to live in
9. Has received a good survey
10. Pleasant neighbours

F. Suppose you had to live in another country, which of these aspects appeal the most?

1. The cost of living
2. Respected in world community
3. Offers more choices in lifestyle
4. Accessible by sea and air
5. Quality of life
6. Population total
7. Beautiful countryside
8. Your friends will love to come and stay

9. A very safe place
to live and work

10. Friendly inhabitants

G. You are choosing a school for your child. Which
criteria are most important to you?

1. The fees
2. School's academic
record
3. A wide curriculum
is available
4. How far it is from
your home
5. Best teaching available

6. Number of pupils
7. Modern/traditional
buildings
8. It is a famous school
9. It is a safe, caring
environment
10. Teachers are
approachable

H. When you shop in a department store, which of these
aspects appeal most?

1. Its prices
2. Its reputation
3. There is a lot of
choice
4. Easy to get to
5. Top-grade goods
on sale
6. How large it is
7. Up-to-date interior

8. Well-known, exclusive
store
9. You can return
unsuitable
items
10. Shop assistants are
helpful and cheerful

## Scoring the questionnaire

Add up the frequency with which you chose the numbered suggestions and record your totals on the scale below.

| | | | |
|---|---|---|---|
| Choice 1 .................... | (Money) | Choice 6 ................. | (Size) |
| Choice 2 .................... | (Reputation) | Choice 7 ................. | (Looks) |
| Choice 3 .................... | (Variety) | Choice 8 ................. | (Popularity) |
| Choice 4 .................... | (Location) | Choice 9 ................. | (Safe decision) |
| Choice 5 .................... | (Quality) | Choice 10................. | (People factors) |

## So - how did you do?

The words used in each of your choices were synonyms of each other (for example: cost of living; fees; price; discounts). Most people find two or three themes recur whenever they are forced to examine a range of criteria in order to make a choice. Surprisingly, this can apply equally to people as well as 'things'. We choose our friends and relationships in the same way as we select a car, an item in a shop or a holiday.

The questionnaire offers you only 10 choices but there are many more common themes which can be important to people when they make a decision. Everyone has their own set of 'hot buttons'. Once developed, these motivators rarely change from decision to decision. If you buy your newspaper from a particular vendor because you like him, you might also live in an area because of the neighbours, choose to work with a friendly group of people. The choices may seem to be different but in fact all can be seen as synonymous.

Some buying motivations are listed below. Alongside each are three synonyms, vague words that can mean the same things to different people.

| MOTIVATION | SYNONYMS | | |
|---|---|---|---|
| **Fast** | Quick | Speedy | Saves time |
| **Safe** | Reliable | Dependable | Guaranteed |
| **Cheap** | Low cost | Inexpensive | Money saving |
| **Reputable** | Name | Image | Make |
| **Well-known** | Advertised | Famous | Popular |
| **Service** | Helpful | Polite | Efficient |
| **Convenient** | Near | Easy | Opening hours |
| **Looks** | Shape | Size | Colour |
| **Fashionable** | Popular | Modern | Current |
| **Prestigious** | Classical | Enviable | First rate |
| **Traditional** | Old style | Dependable | Familiar |
| **Varied** | Choice | Alternatives | Not tied down |
| **Friendly** | Cheerful | Chatty | Comfortable |
| **Performance** | Reliability | Standards | Durability |
| **Unique** | Different | New | Leading edge |
| **Comfortable** | Reliable | Worry free | Peace of mind |

# The psychology of decision-making

*We know what happens to people who stay in the middle of the road. They get run over.*

When asked to make a decision most people have inbuilt sets of strategies they employ instinctively. Ask them why they went for a particular decision and they'll answer: 'I just knew it was the right way to jump.' The chances are high that they make all their decisions the 'right' way. In other words – most of us are locked into a series of perceptual filters that determine what information gets through. Understand another person's strategies and filters and you will clear the way to faster, more binding decisions. Many people seek sensory evidence before making their decisions.

- 'I'd like to *see* some examples first.'
- 'I want to *hear* what Chris thinks about this.'
- 'I want to *read* your report before I decide.'
- 'I have a gut *feeling* about this.'
- 'I need to get a *flavour* of the report first.'

Here are some of the better-known strategies: observing others as they make their choices will help you add more strategies to your collection. Know your quarry well and you will save time and heartache.

## Towards/away

Some people are attracted *towards* something. Salesperson X has a strong drive to get to the top of the sales league and will do practically anything to achieve this. Salesperson Y, however, is repelled *away* from situations. They work hard to *avoid* being demoted or fired.

Both people achieve the same results, but through different motivational channels.

## Internal/external

When Prime Minister Margaret Thatcher was asked 'How does it feel to be out of step with the entire European Union?' she retorted: 'It is they who are out of step with me.' This was a woman entirely at ease with her *internal* voice; immovable, implacable, totally confident. Never mention the thoughts and beliefs of others to the internal decision-maker. In order to persuade them you need to focus on *their* belief system and un-waveringly track it when presenting your case.

An old boss of mine was the opposite. Ask for a decision and he would cast around *externally* for the opinions of others, seeking a consensus before plumping for a final conclusion. So in order to persuade my boss, it was necessary first to lobby those whose opinions he would seek. Get them on your side first, then ask David to make his mind up. Job done.

## Big picture/little picture

It's rare to find someone who has zero curiosity about either the big picture or the little picture. Most people habitually opt for one or the other when making decisions. The big picture person loves large chunks of information and tends to see things globally. They love planning and developing future strategies. Point them in the general direction and they'll find their way. Don't confuse them with the facts. They'll jump to the conclusion on their own, thank you very much.

The little picture person needs to be given a sequence of steps to follow, with sufficient information to support the need for each step.

## Positive/negative

Ask Mrs Positive what she liked about the film you've just seen and she'll catalogue precisely what aspects she liked and how it matched another film. Do the same with Mr Negative and he'll look for a mismatch and tell how he liked such and such a movie better, and how it didn't follow the book.

To persuade Mr Negative to do A rather than B, ask him what it is he doesn't like about B. This will reinforce his need to go for A. And do the reverse with Mrs Positive: 'What is it you like about A?'

## Options/procedures

The options person loves choice and alternatives and doesn't like to be tied down to a single solution. They want to expand their choices. If you fail to provide choices or different ways forward, the options person will feel the need to be creative. So give them plenty of scope for moulding your proposals to their needs, steering them gently towards the finishing line, always letting them feel they are in charge of their destiny.

The procedures person likes to be given a set plan of action and actively dislikes having to develop one of their own. They think there is only one (preferably proven) way to do something. Hopeless at brainstorming alternatives, they want to be told what to do and how to do it, in detail, ideally in writing.

# Establishing decision criteria

Each of us has developed our preferred strategies for making decisions and a variety of (changing) criteria from which we can choose. It is clearly important to consider this when we are seeking approval for our ideas or proposals. But how exactly can we elicit strategies or criteria from people who sometimes have only a vague idea themselves of what it is they are seeking? Short of giving everyone a questionnaire, how can you establish what motivates them? There are several approaches you can take, each depending on circumstances:

- Ask them to tell you what appealed to them about a *similar decision* they have already taken. What factors influenced that decision? Was it the cost? Or perhaps the time frame? Have they carried out a similar project in the past? If so, how successful was it? What made it so successful? (Perhaps it was not a success, in which case find out what it was that prevented it from being a success. If they were dissatisfied, discover why, what went wrong, what would they have preferred?)

- Encourage them to talk you through their preferred strategies. For example: 'When you decide to upgrade a system how do you usually go about it? Do you do this on your own, or after consulting others? Who else do you rely on for advice?' – and so on.

- Talk to people who know them well or those who work alongside them. Ask: 'Have you noticed how they go about making decisions? Who do they usually consult? What seems to be uppermost in their mind as they go about deciding?'

- Ask: 'In what ways will you go about deciding whether my proposition is valid and will work for you?'

## When should you ask for a decision?

If I had a pound for every time I have been asked that question I would be extremely wealthy. There is, of course, no definitive answer. I was once told by a director of a company whose annual sales conference I was about to address: 'Tell 'em to close the sale early and often.' I did not oblige because I feel the old adage 'Always be closing – the ABC of persuasion' is fundamentally flawed.

Suppose you do ask for the decision early. Perhaps before all information has been absorbed, before you have explained the appropriate benefits, before all outstanding objections have been dealt with. Are they likely to provide a resounding 'yes' at this stage?

You opt to ask for a decision as often as you can. The first time you ask, the answer is 'No, I'm not ready to decide.' You ask again a bit later but they are still undecided. Each time you ask, you are forcing them to question earlier refusals to commit. Asking too frequently can only reinforce original reasons for saying 'no' in the first place.

## There's a right time – and a wrong time

So, assuming you don't ask early and avoid asking too often, when is the right time? The right time is when you start to receive *signals* that suggest the person you are trying to influence seems ready to make their decision. When we are mentally prepared to 'go ahead' we give out messages, some conscious others unconscious. Perfect Persuaders seem almost instinctively to know when to get a decision. Many years of practice may have provided them with foolproof but entirely unconscious skills in closing the conversation. If you are a novice or still uncertain of your abilities, you will be consciously observing the other person and noticing what changes take place throughout your dialogue which suggest that now is the right time to ask for a decision.

There are three indications which will tell you that other people may be ready to decide.

### Appropriate body-language signals

Suppose you were buying a wristwatch for a friend's birthday and were unable to decide between three possible choices. Each watch had its own set of attributes, but was different. So difficult, this decision-making. First you picked up one, then another. You put it down and picked up the first again. You thought you noticed a small blemish on the strap and rubbed it gently with your finger. No problem – it came off immediately. The shopkeeper would not need a master's degree in psychology to realise quite early on which of the watches on offer had already become your preferred choice.

The following are body-language signals which may indicate that others are ready to make a final decision. Remember though that one swallow does not make a summer. It may take several signals – separately or in clusters – before you can be certain that it is the right time to go for a decision:

- sitting or leaning forward

- head up, good eye contact

- stroking chin thoughtfully

- nodding

- smiling in agreement

- making notes – especially ticking a list

- knees apart

- feet flat on floor

- hands in open gesture (palms up)

- coat unbuttoned

- upward inflection in voice tone.

## Changes in body language

Apart from the many individual signals, you will also notice subtle (and not so subtle) changes in the other person's body language. Perhaps, when you first mentioned your ideas, the other person was sitting or leaning hard against the back of the chair, feet stretched out in front of them, ankles crossed. Their hands may have been closed or clasped in the shape of a pyramid, or church steeple. Their coat was probably buttoned up and a slight frown or scowl played across their face. You received very little eye contact.

As you progressed, enthusing about your proposal, you noticed a series of changes taking place. The other person seemed visibly to relax. Perhaps it all started when their ankles were uncrossed and their knees drew upwards. The steepled fingers went down on to the desk or on to the tops of their thighs. Their head came up and for the first time they really looked at you.

These changes in body language can be very significant and are strong signals that they are becoming more prepared to listen and even say 'yes' to your proposition. Of course it can just as easily go the other way. Body language that was quite open and positive at the beginning may gradually close and become less responsive and negative. Although you do not need to be a body-language expert to spot these changes, it is quite amazing how many so-called professional salespeople breeze through their day blissfully unaware of any language other than words. And yet body language is as real and far more accurate and significant than the spoken language. Body-language analysis is the art of seeing what others are thinking. Because body signals stem from the subconscious, the signals we see are often a more accurate indicator of feelings and thoughts than carefully chosen words.

## Verbal signals

Verbal signals which suggest that people are ready to say 'yes' are likely to be more direct and unambiguous than the non-verbal. Because the words we use can be vague or ambiguous, it is not always easy to detect the right moment to go for a decision. Be aware of the pace of their conversation with you. If it slows or speeds up it can indicate a readiness to conclude. Some people prefer to listen long and hard before reaching a conclusion. In this case the situation may reverse and you may suddenly find yourself receiving lots of questions.

Here are some examples of ways in which others typically signal verbally that they may be ready to go ahead:

- 'So how soon can you start the project?'

- 'What's the bottom line? How much is this going to cost us, all told?'

- 'Just go through the implementation schedule once more for me.'

- 'Would you be overseeing the project yourself?'

- 'Suppose we want to change things halfway through. Would we be able to?'

- 'Can you guarantee the security of your system?'

- 'Could you redesign it to include some important extras?'

## Testing the water

Although these statements or questions do not explicitly accept your proposals, the last four do contain a number of presumptions and it would be safe to nudge the questioner towards a decision. This is easier than you might think. The final four questions require an answer and it is important to think about the way in which you construct your reply. For example, you could simply say yes to all of these questions: 'Yes we can redesign it'; 'Yes I will be overseeing the project' and so on.

In future whenever you get a leading question from the other person, answer it like this: 'Would you like us to redesign it?'; 'How important is it to you that I oversee the project?'; 'Do you think you may want to make changes partway through?' This is what the salesperson calls a test close. While it does not get you to a final decision, it does reveal how others are thinking, how serious their questions are. Here are some more ways in which you could get a decision.

## Will you marry me? The direct decision question

It should be so easy to simply ask the direct question 'Do you agree?' or 'Shall we go ahead right away?' Yet it is often avoided or left to the very end when more subtle approaches have failed. Its very directness can appeal to the proactive leader and creative talker. It goes like this:

'OK. Shall we go ahead?'
'Fine. Now if there are no more questions I propose that we start on Monday.'

The reason many people avoid this decision question is because it is a closed question. We have been taught so often not to ask closed questions. However, this is precisely the time when you want a yes/no answer. Because they might say 'no', we anticipate an impending sense of rejection and avoid the question altogether.

Nothing could be more dangerous at this stage of influencing. This is a critical moment, it is easy for people to go off the boil. The nettle needs to be grasped – firmly. If you receive a 'no' then you can always ask (PowerQuestion): 'What is it that's preventing you from going ahead?' and quickly elicit the preventative cause.

## Tea or coffee? The alternative choice question

This approach is less direct because you enable people to make a choice between two possible options:

'When would you like to start? Friday, or shall we wait until Monday?'
'Which approach do you prefer?'
'Which film shall we go to see – this one or that one?'
'Would you like tea or do you prefer coffee?'
'Your place or mine?'

The subtlety of this type of question lies in the fact that you are not asking for a direct decision, only for people to make their minds up about an apparent choice that needs to be made. At the very least they cannot reply with a 'no'.

## Oh, just one more thing: The minor decision question

Another soft tactic. With this question you are asking people to make a decision concerning a minor or relatively unimportant aspect of your plan. If they reply positively, then the assumption is that they will agree to everything else you suggest.

'Oh, by the way, where do you think you would like the logo to appear? At the top of the form or do you feel it would look better bottom right?'

'There is one other thing I meant to ask you. How do you plan to fund the project?'

'How do you think we should inform the northern branches?'

'Do you think we should invite your Aunty Maud to the wedding?'

## I'm sure you'll agree: The assumptive decision question

Because this question is assumptive, it implies the other person has already agreed to go ahead. Be careful with this tactic. Analytical listeners and proactive leaders do not like presumption and they will not be afraid to point this out in unequivocal terms. But the assumptive question does work well with the creative talker and the reactive follower, both of whom need continuous nudges towards a final decision.

'After we start, I assume you will want a monthly report on our progress?'

'When we start the project, which improvements will you notice first?'

'Which restaurant shall we go to this weekend?'

## It all adds up: The benefit summary

This works well with people who find it difficult to say yes without a lot of thought (analytical listeners and reactive followers are good examples). They are probably on the brink of saying 'I'd like to give it a bit of thought before saying a final "yes" to the idea.' You can pre-empt this by giving a brief summary of the specific benefits they will gain. When you do this be sure to remind them of their needs in order to reinforce the connection between needs and benefits:

> Before we conclude the meeting I'd like to sum up what we have discussed. I think we all agreed that your main requirements were security and an accurate record of incidents. Am I right? Good. When you install the new system it will be impossible for any clients to log straight in. Only you and your team will have passwords and these will be regularly changed. The client will have to come through your help desk. This in turn will mean you will be able to list all calls and match them against your Service Level Agreements. Assuming you are happy with this solution, I suggest we commence the installation at the end of this month. Is that a good time for you?

It is a long-winded way of getting to 'yes' but worth the effort if you want to be sure that you have covered the ground properly. With dyed-in-the-wool analytical listeners, it would be a shrewd move to follow up your benefit summary in writing so they can mull over your proposal at leisure. Written summaries are useful, too, if your proposals are to be shown to other people. The prime decision-maker may well have others on whose suggestions or agreement they rely. By putting it all in writing you will be able to answer any questions which may arise and need answering in your absence. In other words – don't rely on other people to sell your ideas down the line. They may attempt to do this but are unlikely to make as thorough a job of it as you could.

## Let me tell you a story: The similar situation

How often have you been on the brink of saying yes to a good idea but baulked at the last minute? You may not be the dithery type, but it is perfectly natural to harbour last-minute feelings of doubt or concern about an idea. This is particularly true if you are one of the first people to try out the idea. It is normal to want to leave things for a bit, to let others be the guinea pigs, to allow time to iron out any kinks or get rid of unseen bugs.

As the persuader, you may find all this very frustrating. You have done your job, identified needs, stressed relevant benefits and dealt with all the objections you received. Now it is decision time and this person still doesn't seem prepared to go ahead. What next? It is time to use your empathy. Put yourself in their shoes and ask yourself: 'If I felt as they do, what would help me make a decision? What would I like to hear which would relieve any last-minute doubts and anxieties?'

Tell them about others who have had similar thoughts. Talk them through the sequence of events that led to a final decision. Reassure them that all the doubts and fears vanished after the other person had made the final decision. Tell them how happy this person is with their decision, how they cannot think why they left it so long before making a change. If it is practical, you could put them in touch with others who have made similar decisions. Recall how effective testimonials are when you see them in advertisements. These often favourably contrast a 'before' with an 'after' and allow you to put yourself in others' shoes, to tread the path they have so successfully taken.

# Phew! They said 'yes', now what do I do?

Having gained agreement, it would be easy and potentially fatal to assume that you need do nothing more than rest on your laurels, congratulating yourself on a job well done. After all, they have agreed to your proposition, implementation is under way and at this stage nothing can be lost.

Think again. How often have you suffered from so-called 'buyer's remorse'? You have made a decision to buy something. You are convinced of your needs, you can afford it and what's more – you want it. But mysteriously by the time you reach home you have some serious doubts about your decision. Perhaps you don't really need it. Maybe it was a frivolous decision – you merely wanted it. Anyway it cost a lot – more than you could really afford at this time. What will your partner, colleagues, friends say when you tell them about it?

It is perfectly normal to go through a post-decision depression. As a Perfect Persuader you will want to put some strategies in place for reassuring people that they did after all make the right decision.

Imagine you have successfully convinced a colleague to agree to a simple job share – you do some of their work and they do some of yours. The benefits are straightforward. You will both have more variety within your jobs, you will be able to cover for one another in times of absence. But benefits alone will not necessarily sustain their faith in the idea. Benefits can wear thin after a while.

What can you do or say which will keep your colleague happy and content that they did do the right thing after all?

What will help reinforce their decision:

- on a practical level?

- on an emotional level?

- on a psychological level?

*Customer: Are those eggs fresh?*
*Grocer: Feel the eggs, Henry. See if they're cool enough to sell.*

# 12 Persuading groups of people

*It takes three weeks to deliver a good ad-lib speech.*
Mark Twain, anthor, 1835–1910

There comes a time in most careers when someone says: 'Will you present your findings to the weekly meeting?' Or, 'We have been asked to present a paper at the annual conference. As you have been closely involved you are the person to handle it for us.'

Unfair as it may sound, people in business and social life are often measured by their ability to speak in public. It doesn't seem to matter that you are an expert or have important or useful information about a subject – it is vital that you present it well. The way in which you present and the consequent effectiveness of your influence with the group is critical. Unfair, yes – but critical even so. Of course, knowing this does absolutely nothing to calm our state of mind when we are invited to give the talk. In fact, it usually exacerbates the situation. Most of us feel our stomach looping the loop, our palms running with perspiration and our mouth drying at the mere thought of having to do it. Recent research suggests that there are three common fears which haunt us:

1. speaking to groups

2. heights

3. spiders.

If you are ever invited to speak to airline passengers on the subject of tarantulas I suggest you bow out gracefully. But why is the thought of public speaking such a universal anathema? After all, we have probably been asked to give a talk because we are seen as an expert, someone who has been part of a project and understands it thoroughly, someone who is enthusiastic and knowledgeable, someone who can represent the company/group/department. A large part of the fear we experience can be due to anticipation. We are worried that someone in the audience will know more than we do. We are concerned we may forget something vital or, worse still, dry up altogether. We are frightened at the prospect of being in the spotlight with all eyes focused on us.

## Three ways to minimise fears

There are three ways in which you can get to grips with your fears and phobias. Notice I have used the word 'minimise'. It is unlikely the fear of anticipation will ever leave you entirely. It could be argued that a certain amount of trepidation is desirable. After all, it does suggest we are concerned about the outcome, that we want things to go well. Even the most hardened of professionals feel distinct twinges of adrenaline as they rise to their feet. Ask any of them how they feel about this and they will probably tell you that they use adrenaline to 'fly'. It provides the fuel that will lift them off at the beginning of their talk. And they will also tell you that it dies down and becomes controllable after a couple of minutes or so.

Here then are the three ways you can minimise any fears you may have:

- Prepare and structure your talk before you deliver it. (You would be amazed at the number of people who tell me that they make it all up as they go along. Or who say that they don't want to be tied down to anything too rigidly.)

- Rehearse, rehearse, rehearse. Leave nothing to chance. Get a group of colleagues or friends, sit them down and make them listen to your presentation. Ask for questions, comments, criticism. Prime them to ask you the most difficult questions. Even get them to be rowdy or uninterested if these are the audience reactions you anticipate.

- Recognise you will always feel the fear. Be aware that practically everyone who rises to their feet in front of an audience feels it too. Notice how it slowly fades away as time ticks by. Discover that most of the feelings you have are inside your body and mind. No one can actually see them.

One of the most consistent comments I get when I run presentation-training sessions is: 'Hey, I look a lot better on the videotape than I felt when I was delivering the talk. I don't appear anywhere near as nervous as I felt when I was delivering it.'

Fear is very often a: False Expectation About Reality.

## Anchor the moment

Anchoring is a simple but powerfully effective way of recalling positive resources. Most of us have a piece of music, or a fragrance or taste that takes us immediately back to a past experience. When we hear the music again, smell the fragrance or taste the taste once more, our brain 'thinks' it is back in the past, and the 'anchored' feelings associated with the experience flood once more through our body.

When you are on your feet with your presentation going really well, anchor the moment. Decide on an association (or 'anchor') you want to use to remind you in future of the wonderful feeling of success that is coursing through your system. Choose something you can see, a sound or word you can repeat to yourself and a small, inconspicuous gesture you can make (some people like to dig a fingernail into the ball of their thumb, or touch the points of two fingers firmly together). The memorable image, sound and gesture combine to form your anchor.

When the presentation is complete and the room has emptied, test your anchor. Stand in the room, recall the image and the sound/word you chose and make the inconspicuous gesture. The sensation you anchored – those feelings of confidence and success you experienced during your presentation – should come flooding back and engulf your body and mind.

So, the next time you are on your feet in front of a group and want to re-experience that same feeling of confidence, activate your anchor – the image, word and gesture.

Warning: anchors will fade with time. So during each subsequent successful presentation, reproduce your anchors, exactly as before. They will eventually embed themselves into your system, like that memorable piece of music.

# Planning and preparing to influence groups

Like a lot of things in life, time and effort spent in the planning and preparation phase can be the most valuable investment you will make. Here are some pointers:

- Use your persuasion checklist (see page 7).

- Ask yourself, 'What precisely do I want the group to know, understand or agree to?'

- Because people only listen with 25 per cent efficiency, limit yourself to *three key messages* only. Do not exceed this limit.

- Who is the main decision-maker? Will any subsidiary decision-makers be present?

- How much do they know about the subject?

- What are their needs, requirements, wants?

- Will my ideas fulfil those needs? Can I prove it?

- Can I justify any direct or indirect costs?

- What resistance can I expect? From whom? How will I handle it?

- What approach will suit the group (input from me; questions and answers; detailed handouts; a PowerPoint slide show; plenty of pictures; statistics; drama; demonstration; emotion)?

- What style of influence should I use (autocratic; democratic; logical; emotional; assertive; passive; persuasive; negotiation)?

- How do I plan to gain commitment?

# Mind maps

There are many proven ways of designing the structure of a formal presentation. One of the most common is the so-called mind map. The underlying strength of the formal presentation is that it allows you, the presenter, an opportunity to influence a group of people. If their brains are to relate to your information and be influenced by you, the content of your presentation must be structured so as to slot in as elegantly as possible to their way of thinking. In *The Mind Map Book,* author Tony Buzan says: 'It follows that if the brain works with key concepts in an inter-linked and integrated manner, our notes and our world relations should in many instances be structured in this way rather than in traditional lines. Rather than starting from the top and working down in sentences or lists, one should start from the centre with the main idea and branch out as dictated by the individual ideas and general form of the central theme.'

Mind maps have several advantages over the linear form of lists and note-taking:

- The bulk of notes is significantly reduced.

- Your central idea is more clearly defined.

- The words you choose will be richer in imagery.

- The process of choosing these words involves you more in understanding your material.

- Associating words with ideas will help you recall the key points more readily.

- The more significant ideas and subheadings will be closer to the centre.

- Less important ideas will be nearer the edge.

- The ways in which apparently separate ideas link together will become obvious as the map progresses. This will allow you to make changes in structure quite early on in the map's development.

- Any new ideas can easily be added without altering the general flow.

- Each mind map you create will be unique. This will aid recall and re-use or further development of subsequent presentations.

- Because it allows you to note your ideas in a random fashion, the open-ended structure will help your brain spot new connections more easily.

This is a very practical tool for seeing how your ideas fit together and will provide a simple way of shaping a well-defined structure. It may also provide useful insight into what material you could leave out altogether.

## Example of a mind map

Let us suppose you have been invited to upgrade a computer system for a small family-run business. You have analysed the needs of key individuals and departments and researched the market. You have noted possible anxieties and doubts and have developed counter-arguments. A simple mind map would look something like this:

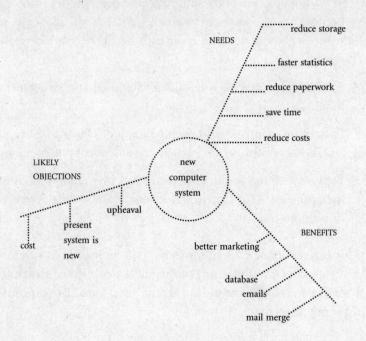

Now you have completed your mind map and can see the wood for the trees, here is an example of a more detailed format for convincing a group to agree to an idea or proposition.

*State your objective:*

• 'I aim to help you choose the most suitable system.'

*Re-cap and agree principal needs:*

- To reduce flow of paperwork between departments and remote offices.

- To provide fast statistical breakdown.

- To develop a just-in-time ordering system.

*List three main benefits of your proposed recommendation:*

- Instant and accurate projections of market requirements will let you know precisely when products will be needed.

- Simple to use formulae and macros will provide continuously updated statistics.

- Email and voicemail will reduce letters and memos within the company.

*Outframe any possible objections:*

- Accept that there may be valid objections to your suggestion and meet them head on.

- Answer these in turn and get agreement that your answers have been accepted.

- Support your solutions to problems and resistance with re-affirmations of your three main benefits.

- If you cannot answer any objections, work hard to minimise their impact on your proposals. Make sure you gain agreement before moving on to:

*Outline 'where we go from here':*

- Organise site visits to similar organisations which already use the system.

- Arrange for your IT people to undergo immersion training in hardware and software usage.

- Set up meetings with the computer company system analysts.

- Dry run the system prior to installation.

- Negotiate system service agreements.

- Agree a provisional installation date.

- Meet and get to know the computer product installation team.

This more formal listing of content now allows you to create your notes. These can range from simple postcard-sized cue cards to larger A5 or even A4 sheets. Most conference presenters like to write everything down as in a speech, highlighting key messages. Others, who use overhead projectors, simply jot a few pointers on the edge of the view foil cardboard frame – each to his own. The key to it all is understanding what strategy works best for you – and sticking to it.

## Establishing rapport with a group

Establishing rapport is arguably the single most important skill needed when persuading others. Influence is sharing information or experience between or among individuals with the aim of bringing about, or avoiding, change. Usually, resistance or barriers to your influence will be present in some form. A sense of mutual rapport between you, the presenter, and your audience will help eliminate many barriers or perceived differences. Having good rapport with your audience will:

- Help you establish and maintain control by staying in constant tune with the prevailing situation; to align with whatever is happening; and to imperceptibly help others change direction or views.

- Help you establish credibility and trust with your audience. Without these you will find it difficult to overcome hostility, anger and resistance to change.

- Help you get others to understand you more clearly. By getting in step with, and understanding how they understand and interpret, their 'reality', you will be able to present your ideas in ways which make good sense to them.

## Rapport with individuals and key players

Good rapport with key players within the group is at least as important as having rapport with the group as a whole. It is highly likely that these key figures will have considerable long-term and overriding influence on the thought patterns and ultimate decisions reached by the group itself. A typical group in a company might contain an interlocking set of individuals. Each individual may have separate thoughts, needs and motives but these could overlap (or even conflict with) others in the team.

Take a typical management structure with individuals who have apparently mutual goals. On closer examination you may find that these goals and aims in fact conflict in some way. This is because they are seen from a different perspective.

Suppose you are planning a presentation where you aim to

persuade colleagues to invest in a new product. You have an audience of around eight or ten that includes the following:

*Managing director*: Entrepreneurial drive for aggressive acquisition of market share and short-term profit growth. Wants to get things agreed quickly and without fuss. Could decide to say 'yes' on the spot.

*Financial accountant*: Has concern for capital investment and the cost of borrowing. Wants to see solid proof and evidence of long-term investment potential. Unlikely to agree without more detail and further meetings.

*Production controller*: Pleased to be able to take up available production capacity. Eager to make a start.

*Sales manager*: Recognises the need to take on more salespeople. Concerned with short-term sales/cost ratio. Doubtful of ultimate value of your proposal.

Clearly, it would not be difficult to convince the MD and the production controller. But if you did convince them, you would be up against the other two, both of whom have equally strong reasons for *not* wanting to go ahead. You may be lucky and the managing director might simply line up with production and railroad the decision through in favour of your ideas. Autocracy wins the day. But, equally strongly, this path may create dissatisfaction in the minds of the accountant and the sales manager. Feeling miffed that their protestations have been ignored, they may well work covertly to sabotage the final outcome. And they are well placed to do this.

This is where your rapport skills come in. Using your empathy, putting yourself in the shoes of all four individuals, you will start to see things as they do. Early rapport with the financial accountant and sales manager will incorporate their concerns and alleviate some of these early on in the presentation.

A simple checklist of ways to gain/maintain rapport with different people in the group might contain some of the following (this list is not exhaustive as different circumstances and group mixes will demand different approaches):

- Shake hands with all or as many people as time or size of group allows.

- Acknowledge them by name, title or discipline whenever appropriate.

- Establish early eye contact with key players and secondary influencers.

- Mention the title or value of their job function as often as possible.

- Reaffirm their personal needs throughout the presentation.

- Acknowledge their possible doubts and fears and reassure them you understand.

## Rapport with the whole group

Groups are dynamic and moods and attitudes can swing quite rapidly from positive to negative, or vice versa. As a presenter your antennae must be constantly quivering, watching out for those subtle and not so subtle changes that could signal important shifts in the collective outlook of the group.

- Watch people's body language. Notice significant changes.

- When changes occur, do something different. Speed up, slow down. Sit down, ask for questions. Suggest a short comfort break. Talk louder, faster, slower. Break off and recount a (pertinent) anecdote. Invite relevant experiences that will confirm your main message.

- Let the group know that you recognise the part they play in a corporate identity: 'As residents of Willow Park Estate, you will all know only too clearly . . . '

## Using PowerPoint

Many presenters hide behind a presentation that relies heavily on Microsoft's PowerPoint. You can stand, back to the group, gesturing wildly at some bullet point or graphic. And it's handy to have a slide on the screen at all times – you can be sure that the group will be examining its contents, not you and your nerves.

Wrong. Slide presentations should be used when specific (not general) points require *emphasising* by you or *memorising* by your audience. They should be supported by detailed handouts (given to the audience at the conclusion of the presentation).

PowerPoint offers you the luxury of a pre-designed template, background and layout. You can add pictures, graphics and text and even a motion clip and sound effects. The danger is that your audience will be so thoroughly familiar with the look of your slides that they'll turn off, rather than on to, your exciting subject matter.

A few rules:

- Restrict your slides to an absolute maximum of six bullet points (three is even better).

- Each bullet-point message ideally to be no longer than five words.

- Use a large sans serif font, clearly readable at the back of the room.

- Use colours sparingly (an estimated nine to twelve per cent of the male population suffers from some form of colour blindness).

- Use simple graphics to illustrate contrasting statistics.

- Minimise the number of slides used. Try to get away with three. (Your audience will remember the beginning and end of your presentation. Too many slides will leave them reeling from information overload).

- Remember how you felt and reacted when you last sat through an interminable presentation. Dare to be different and your audience will love you for it – and agree to your proposition more readily.

## Future pacing

Future pacing is a technique which invites the audience to imagine a situation in the future where the knowledge they are gaining from your presentation will be useful.

One way to achieve this is to allow your audience to *visualise* a future situation unfolding and to *imagine* their new skills or knowledge being used successfully. Another approach is to extend the imagined scenario by getting your audience to imagine how they will *feel* when they have achieved something, or to *hear* other people congratulating them on their achievement. Mental rehearsal is practice in the imagination and helps to anchor learning and understanding.

## Presupposition

Presupposition uses words and phrases which presuppose that some thing or event will take place in the future.

- 'When you get back to your office and find yourself using this information . . . '
- 'You will discover that these ideas will be . . . '
- 'Shall we break now or in 15 minutes?'

## Embedded commands

Messages woven into other messages which have a specific and intended outcome. It is possible to command your audience to do something you want, or to control their reaction to your suggestions: 'Although I will be giving handouts at the end of my presentation, you may like to . . . *take notes as we go* . . . which will supplement my handout material.'

More oblique uses of the embedded command include: 'When you use these ideas *successfully* in your work . . .'; 'Although you feel that . . . *I have covered everything* . . . there may be a *couple of quick questions* . . . some of you would like to ask before we . . . *go into lunch*.'

## Analogy

Analogy is one of the most useful communication tools. It can help your audience grasp something in 10 seconds which may ordinarily take them 60 or 90 seconds to understand. It's as easy

as ABC to use: 'The form is very *similar to* the car tax document';
'The software is rather *like* a basic word-processing package . . . '

## Metaphor

Since time began people have told stories to one another. In all
parts of the world the story still has enormous significance in
helping us to form a view of life. Too many presentations and
meetings are dry and laboured. Audiences often crave a little excitement, fun or emotion. At first sight this may seem out of place in
the context of a formal meeting or presentation. But how often
have you noticed how effective laughter can be as an ice-breaker?
People instantly relax and seem somehow more compliant and
open to suggestion.

Metaphor is an elegant way of telling a story which contains a
hidden message. In *Steps to an Ecology of Mind,* Gregory Bateson
tells of a man who wanted to know about the mind. What was it?
Would computers ever be as intelligent as humans? The man
entered the following question into the world's most powerful
computer: 'Do you compute that you will ever think like a human
being?'

The computer coughed and spluttered, rumbled, went quiet for
a long time, then printed out its reply. The man tore it out of the
printer in great excitement and read the following words: 'That
reminds me of a story . . . '

Metaphors are used widely by therapists to effect change in their
clients' beliefs or state of mind. This is because the client believes
quite firmly they have a clear grip on reality. To talk to them in
the own language will generally result in circular and repetitive
dialogue, using the same language patterns and descriptive terms.
(Have you ever noticed how domestic arguments often follow an

almost ritualistic pattern, from the first words through to the inevitable conclusion?) Therapists have found that one neat and simple way to *apparently* talk about the client's 'reality' is to use metaphor, stories, jokes, parables, experiences or other examples. This allows the therapist to make small but significant changes in the way the story is told. By doing this he or she changes its perspective and the perspective of the client. Once this has taken place, it is often a simple matter to reframe the background and causes of the problem and thus its potential for change and eventual resolution.

On a more basic level, metaphor can sound something like: 'I recall how difficult it was as a child to learn tables. It seemed completely impossible. But slowly I started to put them into my unconscious mind so that now when someone says "four sevens", I don't need to *think* of the answer – it just comes.' Followed by: 'So even if you find some of my material a little difficult to understand now, *in the future* when you *use it successfully,* you will discover it comes naturally from your unconscious mind.' (Note the added presupposition and embedded command in the last sentence.)

## Powerful presentation words

Top presenters, speakers, teachers and trainers use the words *you, we* and *I* extensively. They include the audience at all times in what they are saying or doing. For instance: 'You and I both know that this makes sense, don't we?' enrols the audience into the assumption that what is being suggested *does* make sense.

Yale University studied 'power words' and concluded that the most effective words were those which affect us most directly. Some examples are: you, easy, love, free, positive, most, save, discover, health, success, will, greatest, proven, results, new, guaranteed, safe, best, how, pleased, when, tested, unique, excellence, how to, announcing, now, win, I wonder if, power.

With your new list of words you have proven success tips that are easy to use. You will find yourself using them in future presentations in different combinations with positive results.


## Anchoring parts of the room

As we learned earlier, an anchor is any powerful stimulus – response mechanism. For example, some people get hungry just by walking into their kitchen. You can use this powerful tool in your presentations to increase understanding, acceptance and empathy with your audience.

As a presenter you wear many hats – for example, you may be casual, friendly, chatty. Some of the time you may want to be particularly dramatic, or serious. Then again, you may want to make explicit suggestions or give orders to the audience. Some of the time you will be presenting cold facts, other times you will want to interact with the audience or make an announcement.

When you are being particularly serious, for example, you will speak in a different tone and pace your message in a special way. You could also go to another part of the room to speak from, thus *anchoring* the spot to what you are saying. Throughout your presentation, whenever you want to place special emphasis on a message you can move back to the same place in the room, pause and make your points. Subconsciously, your audience will understand the significance of this ritual as it happens and will be far more susceptible to suggestions made from that part of the room.

(A typical example of this is the speaker who sits quite casually on the front edge of the desk to make general administrative announcements, but then moves behind the desk, stands and speaks louder and more slowly when starting the presentation proper.)

## Gaining group agreement

There were two prime reasons why you convened this group to hear your ideas:

1. To influence them to do something.

2. To persuade them to agree to do it.

The route to agreement can be fraught with danger and frustration. You think you have convinced them when someone at the back asks: 'Have you thought about the northern division? How will they feel about your idea?' Your audience looks at one another and nods significantly. A murmur rises, becomes a babble and you realise you have lost your grip. You have been heading down one route and the guy at the back has been on an entirely different path.

When you commute to a well-known destination you will have some alternative routes in mind. This is in case there are unforeseen delays or hold-ups. You check the map and memorise possible alternatives. It is the same when you present. You have a destination (group agreement with your ideas) and similarly you will need to have several possible routes to success.

## Use PowerQuestions

When a participant at your meeting or presentation says 'We cannot do that', do not ask why. Simply seek the apparent preventative cause by asking : 'What exactly is it that prevents you from doing it?'

Risk is about breaking from the past. It is possible you are asking the group to make a risk calculation or assessment. Many in the group will want to stick with the status quo, preferring the known to the scary unknown. A useful PowerQuestion to ask your audience is: 'What will happen if we don't change?' What will be the consequences of inactivity? How will this affect our standing in a competitive market place? In what ways will risks we take be counterbalanced by benefits gained?

Question carefully the motives of people who seem to take delight in scuppering your plans at the last minute. Why didn't they introduce their doubts earlier on? Why have they waited until the end before trying to sink your proposal? If it seems appropriate, ask the rest of the group or audience: 'How do you feel about Chris's thoughts? Do you agree with them?' A quick head count will reveal the strength of feeling within the group. It is often the case that those who introduce last-minute doubts are unsure of the benefits of your proposal or simply flexing their muscles in front of peers or superiors. But be careful. You may win this argument but unless it is handled carefully you may find that the boat-rocker manages subsequently to reverse the situation.

# 13  Persuading on the telephone

It has been said that human beings spend 80 per cent of their waking hours communicating with others. Thirty per cent of this time is devoted to talking while 50 per cent is listening. And yet within one hour of holding a conversation it is estimated that over half of what we just heard is forgotten or at best open to gross misinterpretation. With so many of us owning a telephone and with so few of us receiving any formal training in its use it is easy to understand why this special means of communication can be badly handled. We can't live without it but perversely the telephone can become our worst enemy. There are five key causes of additional potential communication problems when we use the telephone:

1. We have no visual clues.

2. We can lose control of the conversation.

3. Telephone conversations are expected to be brief.

4. It is easy to become distracted.

5. The telephone is widely regarded by many as an intrusion.

# Lack of visual clues

In some respects the fact that we cannot see the person we are talking to on the telephone can be a positive advantage. When we talk face-to-face our senses are bombarded with information. We see so many things which are unconnected with the conversation subject matter. Another person walks by, a door opens and closes, a bus parks outside the window. Not serious distractions perhaps, but distractions even so. In some respects, therefore, by isolating the words people say, the telephone has a singular advantage over other means of influence.

However, when we persuade someone to make a decision we support our proposition with appropriate benefits. Without access to that person, without seeing them in their surroundings, it can be difficult to relate benefits directly to their circumstances or value and belief system. When we make a point, how do we know for certain that the other person really agrees with it? The subtle non-verbal clues that accompany all our communications with the world are simply not there. So when the other person says 'yes' how can we be sure that they don't mean 'maybe' or even 'no'?

Over the last 25 years a great deal of attention has been paid to 'relationships': 'Ours is a people business'; 'The customer is king'; 'Customer satisfaction is everything'. The emphasis is now less on what we influence others to do but more on how well we are able to relate to others. It is essential that the telephone environment that we create is structured by the values, beliefs, needs and wants of the other person. There is a strong case to be made for several short telephone calls rather than one long one. Taking time to get to know the other person (or if we already know them, to reinforce the relationship) can pay handsome dividends. Merrill Lynch, the financial management and advisory company, conducted a study and found that the prime reason why a customer chose a broker was that they liked the person they were dealing with. Honesty and trust came second and third. Lastly was the ability to make money.

Before you pick up the telephone to convince someone, ask yourself this question: 'Which is most important to me – to convince the other person or to get them to agree with me?'

There is a subtle difference. To wish to convince the other person means that you are focused on the content of your message, on your outcome rather than theirs. To persuade them to agree with your ideas means that you are focusing on them the person, on their needs, fears, aspirations.

## Using your voice to develop rapport on the telephone

Telephone communication can be summed up as 'What you say and how you say it.' When we think of 'the voice' we tend to restrict our thoughts to voice tone. When striving to gain rapport there is much more to be achieved through our voices than simply tone:

- We can adjust the rate at which we speak.

- We can control the volume at which we speak.

- We can choose the words we use when we speak.

Before looking at these three important variables let's examine the importance of voice tone. Research suggests that voice tone contributes a colossal 38 per cent to the total message we present. The emphasis we choose to place on each and every word we say can radically alter the perceived meaning of our communication.

For example, take a simple statement: 'I would like you to have the report ready for Friday's meeting.' In how many ways can we alter the meaning or shift the emphasis of this simple clause:

'*I* would like you to have the report ready for Friday's meeting.'
'I *would* like you to have the report ready for Friday's meeting.'
'I would *like* you to have the report ready for Friday's meeting.'
'I would like *you* to have the report ready for Friday's meeting.'
'I would like you to have *the report* ready for Friday's meeting.'
'I would like you to have the report *ready* for Friday's meeting.'
'I would like you to have the report ready for *Friday's* meeting.'
'I would like you to have the report ready for Friday's *meeting*.'

One statement – eight tonal variants giving eight substantially different emphases of meaning and intent. How often have you heard the words 'very urgent' and been able to tell precisely *how* urgent by registering the emphasis placed on 'very' or 'urgent'?

## Controlling your rate of speech

There are fast speakers and there are slow speakers. The fast speakers tend to think that slow speakers are irritatingly hesitant, fumbling for words and putting the listener way ahead of the conversation. On the other hand, the slow speakers simply cannot cope with the torrent of words coming down the line. Are you fast or slow? Do you adjust your rate of speech to match precisely that of the person you are trying to influence? It is so easy to do, yet so easy to overlook. This is a subtle and totally effective way of matching and gaining early rapport with a person you may never have met and certainly cannot see. Even if the other person is verging on the hysterical, gabbling their sentences and falling over their words, it is still perfectly possible to match them in volume and speed. Then, imperceptibly to slow down the rate and reduce the volume until you are speaking quite levelly and normally, noticing at the same time how control of your state has affected theirs.

## Controlling the volume of your voice

For many people the volume at which they speak is used to signal their mood. At a time of sadness or mourning it is normal and socially appropriate to speak quietly. On the other hand, this approach would appear unusual at a party or large social gathering. Some people become quite quiet and speak with a calm regularity when they are angry or displeased. Others let rip and shout. As you begin to notice the different ways in which others conduct themselves, how they use their voice volume as a platform to support messages or moods, notice too how this affects you. Are you intimidated by those who shout or talk loudly? Do people who speak quietly and calmly only succeed in irritating you?

Matching volume of speech can be a slightly scary thing to try if you have not done it before. At first glance it seems counter-productive to yell back at someone who is blasting off at you. But put yourself in their shoes for a moment. How might they feel if you remain cool and calm? They would rightly think that there is a mismatch just as they would if they were happy and positive when you were the opposite.

Why match speech at all? Why is it so important? Because it is a prelude to *leading the other person where you want them to go*. People who speak loudly and forcefully can be led quickly towards a quieter and calmer mood. Here's how it might sound:

Them (*loudly*): I do not agree with you and that is final.
You (*same volume*): Yes, and I can see your point of view. (*Slightly*

*quieter*) What we need to do is find out where the differences lie and sort things out. (*Even quieter*) I am sure that you will agree that we can both gain if we can settle these minor points.

Them (*Far quieter*): Well yes. I suppose you're right. So, what exactly do you propose?

Of course in real life this dialogue may well last longer. If you fail to match and lead, go back to the original volume and do it again. You will eventually succeed.

## Matching words and speech patterns

Matching words and speech patterns is simple and subtle. As an experiment listen to professional radio presenters. With only one channel (auditory) through which to express themselves they usually speak economically and expressively. Listen for a few minutes then mimic the presenter. Notice how different this is from how you would normally say the same thing.

We humans see the world from our own singular viewpoint. We spend large portions of our day describing to others this 'reality' as we see it. As our 'reality' is only a personal perception it is often difficult and even counterproductive to attempt to alter it. In order to step inside other people's 'reality' it is important to use their methods of describing it. For instance, they may use adjectives such as: beautiful, large, nice. Or adverbs like: quickly, easily, approximately. Close analysis of these six words reveals absolutely nothing. What do they mean, exactly? What is 'nice'? How approximate is 'approximately'?

Unless you really need to know the precise meaning of these descriptive words, do not bother to use a PowerQuestion – simply use the same word, in your response:

Them: We want to get this done quickly.
You: So doing it quickly is important to you?

The use of so-called speech patterns is very similar. Many of us
have pet phrases that we use frequently. We know what we mean
when we use these words. Here are some examples:

> 'Know what I mean?'
> 'I hear what you say.'
> 'To be honest.'
> 'So I went: "You did what?"'
> 'Yep. OK. Got it.'
> 'Right. Sure. Fine.'

There is often a link between preferred speech patterns and personality. For instance, the proactive leader may use 'Yep, OK, got it' to
suggest a quick mind, or a need to move on. The strong silent analytical listener may say: 'Hmm, yes I believe I know what you mean
and fully concur with your point of view.' The jolly creative talker
often uses phrases such as: 'I'm pretty pleased to hear that. Great,
let's talk more.' The dithery reactive follower, on the other hand, will
be less outgoing, less garrulous: 'Er, I'm a bit unsure of that last point.
Would you mind very much just going over it once more. Sorry.'

Listen and match whenever it is appropriate. You do not have
to copy slavishly, merely echo what you hear. People like people
who are like themselves.

# Telephone words to use

Short words used in short sentences suggest direct action. Long
rambling phrases backed up by a flood of subordinate clauses

merely generate confusion, if you get my meaning, I mean most of us do it from time to time, well maybe not most but certainly lots do, I expect you've seen that haven't you, it's all too common these days, and it's really easy to lose your way within a conversation if you're not very careful.

I hope the point is made. Most adults experience increasing difficulty in following the sense if a spoken sentence is of more than 18 words.

## Using names on the telephone

It is becoming more common in the Western world to talk on first name terms with people we have never met. The Microsoft Corporation recently experimented with a new telephone sales service in the United Kingdom. Their operators greeted callers by saying: 'Good morning, thank you for calling Microsoft Connection, you're through to Alex, how may I help?' Analysis showed that on average over 40 per cent of callers immediately replied using their own first name: 'Good morning, my name is Richard Storey and I was wondering if . . . ' 'Thank you for calling, Richard. If I can be of further help you can reach me on extension 4951 – just ask for Alex.'

Some love this approach, others hate it. The trick is to gauge correctly by listening to the way the other person chooses to introduce themselves. Then match it. It is useful to refer to others by name at the beginning of the conversation, maybe once or twice during it and definitely at the end. But do not fall into the trap of overusing names of people you do not know on the telephone. After a while it becomes obvious and very off-putting.

# 14 Persuading in writing

The need to influence others in writing is generated in virtually every public and private business sector. Every day businesses throughout the world generate countless millions of letters, emails, faxes, reports and proposals. Although English is the most common business language in use, different applications, spelling and usage create an immense potential for international misunderstanding. The United States is the largest national group of English-speakers, outnumbering the rest of the native English-speakers of the world. Waves of British immigrants took English to Africa, Australia, New Zealand and other parts of what was known as the British Empire. Written English in these countries (including India, Hong Kong, Malaysia, Jamaica, Belize and Bermuda) has generally maintained conventional British usage.

If your document is to be seen in another country, make quite sure that as far as possible it conforms to the expectations of the local reader. Nothing is more likely to develop resistance in your reader than ignorance of local convention.

## Eight steps towards more convincing reports and proposals

1. Shake hands with your readers. Always incorporate a covering letter (or email/memo if the report is for internal consumption).

2. Emphasise your credentials.

3. As far as possible within the constraints laid down in the terms of reference, write in your own style.

4. Length proves nothing. There are no rules which state how long a manuscript should be. It should be as long as is necessary to make your points. But no longer.

5. Although reports and proposals are conventionally written in an impersonal style, for example, 'It will be appreciated that', 'It has been concluded that', it is better to try and connect with the reader more directly. Try 'As you can see' or 'As engineers you will understand only too well . . . '

6. Put some sell into your report title: 'Improving efficiency through XYZ'.

7. Short reports (12 pages or less) do not require tables of contents, appendices and so on.

8. Don't overdress the document. Embossed leather with gold tooling may sell a dictionary but your proposal needs only a simple line drawing or illustration.

## Style

Style is usually dictated by the internal approach adopted by the organisation you work in, or the person or organisation to whom you are writing. Solicited proposals often demand that quite strict conventions of layout, style and content are to be followed to the letter. This approach, while easy to conform to, allows little or no opportunity for individuality in writing style.

As a general rule, style should conform to the A, B, C of written English:

A – be accurate
B – be brief
C – be clear.

Accuracy is clearly a vital component of written material. If in conversation you say something that is inaccurate, others will point out the error or you will quickly correct yourself. Once you have written inaccuracies it is impossible to redeem the situation. They are there for all to see for evermore – in writing, with your name at the bottom. Check, double-check and check once more to remove anything that is wrong, does not add up or is a misprint or typo. Brevity is another quite critical aspect of writing. It is a commonly held belief that the length of a document is somehow indicative of the amount of time or effort that has been invested in its creation. This may be the case – but the average readers (especially those at the top) do not have the time to plough through fat reports. They want to know what you are recommending, your basic conclusions, the cost and the implementation schedule. The ways and means of arriving at these are generally of little importance to the busy reader. If your document is more than a few pages long, create a short 'executive summary' to accompany the main report. (This will get a high readership for your report as everyone likes to think of themselves as an executive!)

Clarity in writing style is all about simplicity and directness. Take these two extracts as an example (both adapted from actual reports):

> *Careful consideration has been given by the members of the subcommittee to the question of whether it is in any*

*way necessary or desirable that new legislation should be passed in order to facilitate the transfer of public house licences into newly developed urban neighbourhood areas, so as to follow the consequent movement of populations.*

*Traditional centres of pedagogical training were not all taken by surprise by the contemporary socio-economic challenges of the new millennium. The catalogue of changes that have occurred in them during the current decade is impressive evidence of their ability to make important adjustments required by new situations. To what extent, however, such innovative adjustments have sufficiently replaced older habits or contributed to the sociological reorientation of teacher training is an open question. It may take more time than we think for these adjustments to reveal their total cumulative significance.*

In the first extract there are several features that contribute to a lack of clarity:

- The sentence is too long. Keep sentences at 18 words or less on average.

- There are too many unnecessary words ('Careful consideration has been given by the members of the subcommittee' could easily be reduced to 'The subcommittee considered . . .').

- There is no punctuation to assist the reader.

- The subject '. . . transfer of public house licences . . .' appears after the object '. . . new legislation . . .' This is a common problem, known as 'subject–object inversion' and can confuse the reader. A simple sentence comprising noun/verb/object, such as 'The cat sat on the mat', can be radically altered if the subject and object are inverted – 'The mat was underneath the cat'.

The second extract also lacks clarity but for different reasons:

- There is an overuse of long words. 'Traditional centres of pedagogical training' could just as easily be called 'Old-style teacher training colleges'.

- Adjectives are added to most of the key nouns – '*impressive* evidence', '*important* adjustments', '*innovative* adjustments'. In many cases these could be dropped without affecting the general sense and meaning of the paragraph.

- It has a pompous tone – one teacher writing to impress another?

In order to check the clarity of your writing you can either show it to a friend or colleague whose opinion and judgement you value, or use one of the many grade level indices contained in word processors. A well-known index which you can easily apply to your own written material is called the Fog Index (or Factor). The word 'fog' in this case refers to clarity of style. Devised in the United States, this results in an index which relates to the minimum reading age required to absorb the writing with ease.

## Calculating the Fog Index

To calculate your Fog Index, take a passage of around 100 words (this should contain no quotations). Divide by the number of sentences, giving average sentence length. Call this total A. Now total the number of words which have three or more syllables (avoiding proper names or nouns and any words which have prefixes or suffixes which increase their length to three syllables e.g. creat*ed*; amount*ing*; *re*arrange). Call this total B.

Adding totals A and B and multiplying by a factor of 0.4 will give the Fog Index. The final figure approximately represents the minimum reading age required by your reader in order to make immediate sense of your written passage. For instance, British news-papers have the following typical Fog Index range: *Sun* 6–8; *Daily Express*, *Daily Mail* 10–12; *Daily Telegraph*, *Guardian*, *The Times* 14–18; *Independent* 20–4.

Complex material containing technical terms can be made easier to read by reducing the average length of your sentences. If your sentences of more than 18 words are made longer by the addition of subordinate clauses, you can reduce the Fog Index by cutting down polysyllabic words.

## You *can* tell a book by its cover

One of my clients manufactures aircraft instrumentation and is frequently asked to bid for business, usually against competition from Germany and the United States. Although the structure of the proposals themselves is strictly geared to an agreed format, the look of the actual covers of the proposals was not specified. For a time my client would design quite lavish covers – glossy full colour photographs of fighter plane cockpits with jazzy head-up displays roaring past mountains of cumulus cloud. Then they had a visit from the Ministry of Defence. They were told to restrict future covers to plain blue with black print.

What does this tell you about the power of presentation? Clearly the MOD were aware that the content of my client's proposals might have become secondary to the *look* of the proposals themselves. However, a flashy and expensive proposal will not necessarily win business. A sloppy and carelessly written bid will most definitely contribute to lost business.

- If your company sells computer equipment, use a drawing or photograph of the equipment or a person or people operating it.

- If your product is a service, use line drawings or photographs of people performing or receiving your service.

- If your company provides software products, an overprinted copy of the output as it will apply to the reader would be interesting.

## Physical organisation

A large part of the process of influencing people in writing is to make things easy for the reader. One client of mine once wrote a lengthy report to his board and out of a sense of perversity, or just plain ignorance, decided not to summarise his recommendations. They were there, all right, but scattered throughout the text. This strategy forced his readers to search out his recommendations or even to read the whole text in order to find out what they were (rather like a murder mystery). As the report had taken several months to compile it was a long document and my client asked me to give him feedback, in particular to answer the question: 'After nearly nine months why haven't I had any feedback from the board?'

The answer was simple – he had not attempted to make life easy for his important readers. He imagined that they would rush home clutching his exciting report to their bosoms, eager to get tucked up in bed early for an engrossing read. Not so. Probably what happened was that the board members took one look at the report and passed it down the line to some poor assistant for appraisal. In any event the report, its findings and secret recommendations sank without trace.

## The executive summary

An executive summary is a key tool for influencing readers who may not have the time or inclination to read your whole report. It has little to do with product presentation, but everything to do with a Perfectly Persuasive sales pitch. It is far more than an abstract that merely presents the rest of the document – it represents a unique opportunity to convince your readers that your solution provides the best value proposition: the best benefit at the lowest cost.

The more technical your proposal, the more important the executive summary. Unlike the abstract, the executive summary steers clear of technicalities, concentrating instead on summarising and validating the benefits for the reader. It should include:

- a concise description of how your proposals address the agreed needs of the reader

- a brief narrative version of your proposals

- information primarily about customer (benefits), not about you or your product (features)

- brief mention of any assumptions which you may have made

- minimal technical detail

- little or no technical jargon

- strong, enthusiastic and proactive language

- no detailed breakdowns of pricing information, but an overall cost figure may be appropriate

- brief, details of implementation requirements and timings (only brief, as these will be outlined in full elsewhere in your report).

## Page layout

Reduce clutter and make your report as readable and visually pleasing as you can. Wide margins, double spacing, indentations, bullet points, a clear (preferably decimal) numbering system, plenty of illustrations – all go towards improving readability.

## Illustrations

Many a good argument is wasted because the writer failed to recognise ways in which it could be reinforced by valid illustrations and tables. These can be invaluable if you are:

- making comparisons between two courses of action or the past versus the present (or future)

- writing for readers who are used to or prefer to see pictorial representations

- reinforcing sales messages subliminally, for example, happy smiling users operating your machinery.

# Anticipating and dealing with objections

Someone once described sales proposals as misleading arguments attempting to reach foregone conclusions. Many reports, sales letters and proposals do read that way. It is worthwhile admitting any obvious flaws in your argument at the outset and then setting out how you propose removing or minimising them. The main fallacies that could trip you up are:

- oversimplification
- false analogy
- use of ambiguous words
- use of misleading illustrations
- potted thinking
- sweeping statements
- reaching false conclusions
- misleading the reader through conscious omission
- introducing irrelevant matter into the argument
- assuming points which have been taken for granted.

# Business letters

Dull, clichéd, assumptive and unfriendly – these are just a few of the accusations levelled at business letters. 'Ah, yes,' one client told me, 'but we can't do anything about them as they are on our word-processor.' What a fallacious argument. Who composed the word-processed letters in the first place? Another word processor? And who says that they cannot be altered, improved or ditched altogether?

First, axe the clichés. Whenever you use a cliché you are using someone else's style, not your own. Most of the following expressions are avoidable – try to substitute a more direct or friendly alternative:

- advise us as to

- it is our understanding that

- we acknowledge receipt of

- are not in a position to

- see our way clear to

- may rest assured

- in the event

- at which time

- we are of the opinion

- in view of the fact

- in the near future

- give consideration to

- we are returning herewith

- with reference to

- in connection with.

If you want a perfect model of clarity, succinctness and persuasiveness then study the sales letters sent out in their millions by

Reader's Digest, American Express and Time-Life. Whenever I mention these on my training courses the groans can be heard a mile off. Everyone says they ignore these letters and usually throw them away unopened. This may well be the case. But why do these sales letters make the companies among the richest in the world? Why do their letters get such a high response? Study them again and model them for clarity and success.

Finally, always finish your letter with a clear statement of what it is that you want your reader to do next. Never leave them in doubt. This is arguably the most important part of your letter – the action line.

# The next steps

Once upon a time there was a man and wife. They had achieved many of their ambitions in life, but one important goal remained outstanding. They wanted to swim to Japan.

They discussed this and one day set off. Not practised swimmers, at first they found it difficult. They were aware of how heavy their limbs felt. They ached with the constant effort, especially when the current was against them. Gradually, however, their bodies got used to swimming and they developed a style that became effortless and rhythmical. They learned how to find food in the water, how to nourish themselves and how to use their bodies effortlessly.

Their senses became more attuned to the water around them, how it changed colour as the days went by. And they became aware of the creatures in the water; the small silver fish that swam with them; the dark shadows that skimmed by them in the deep. They became aware of how the sound of the waves changed as they lapped their ears, and they felt the subtle changes of the weather as breezes turned into winds and died down again. They developed a refined sense of smell and could detect tiny changes in the environment by the scent carried to them on the breeze.

They swam for days and weeks with no sign of land on the horizon. They swam on and on until one morning they recognised the shoreline of Japan. As they approached they became quiet and eventually they knew. At that moment, they turned back to the sea and swam on.

# The cycle of mastery

Like the couple swimming to Japan, it will take time for you to become an unconsciously competent Perfect Persuader. And when you do, what then? It can be too easy to drop back, become lazy and complacent. It is at this stage that the learning has only just commenced.

In judo, the beginner starts with a white belt and progresses through many stages until the much-desired black belt is awarded for the peak of achievement. But beyond the peak there are other peaks to conquer. So, on completing the full circle of judo, as of life, the expert returns to the white belt: where they first started.

Learning never stops. Successful sports people practise the same shots and moves over and over to keep their skills 'in the muscle'. They constantly question their assumptions about competence, returning over and over to the basics. The throwaway term 'easy to master' is an oxymoron – a contradiction in terms. Mastery is not simple. You can never be elegant enough.

> *Your future is not a result of choices among alternative paths offered by the present, but a place that is created by you; created first in your mind and will, created next through your activity. Your future is not a place you are going to, but one you are creating.*

Although the subtle art of persuasion is, in part, genetically inbuilt, I am confident that you will already have begun to notice how this book has altered your perspective; how the tools and techniques you have learned are gradually impacting on the way in which you interact with those around you: loved ones, friends, relations, neighbours, colleagues.

As a Perfect Persuader you will want to share what you have

learned and at the same time observe how other people are different. While enthusiasm is contagious be aware that it can also be self-defeating. To make a difference you have to deal with people as they are, now, not as you think they ought to be.

In persuasion, as in all other aspects of human behaviour, it is the difference that makes the difference. You (and those around you) will soon notice differences in your approaches to persuasion: how your objectivity has become more focused, your rapport skills have softened, your sensory acuity has sharpened, your flexibility and range of skills have broadened. Perfect Persuaders are fun to be around. They are in turns strong, decisive and highly motivating. Doors seem to open for them, relationships somehow develop for them, success magically beckons.

Now that you know all about Perfect Persuasion, what are you going to do with the information? Please let me know about your successes and achievements – the highlights of your continuing development. I look forward to hearing from you. Please email your successes, thoughts, questions, requests to: sigmatrainingservices@googlemail.com

# Quick reference 1
# Perfect Persuader's checklist

Use or adapt the following checklist to help plan your systematic approach to persuasion:

*Step one:* Background details of my forthcoming scenario. (Whom will I be persuading? Are they the decision-maker or one of a group of decision-makers? What will I be persuading them to do or think? When will I carry out my dialogue? Will it take one meeting or many? Where will I conduct the meeting? What will be the advantages/disadvantages of different locations?)

*Step two:* My specific objectives. (What outcomes do I want? What is the best – worst – most likely outcome?)

*Step three:* What do I know about the values and beliefs, needs and wants of the decision-maker?

*Step four:* How will the other person benefit from my proposition?

*Step five:* Which persuasion style will work best? Which style will be least productive?

*Step six:* What are the other person's typical (or probable) decision-making strategies?

*Step seven:* What is their personality like and how might it affect my strategy and tactics?

*Step eight:* What is my strategy for developing/maintaining good rapport?

*Step nine:* What objections am I anticipating? How do I plan to overcome them?

*Step ten:* How do I plan to get a decision?

## Quick reference 2
# Some suggested sources of inspiration

Now that you are well on the way to becoming a Perfect Persuader, the time has come to look at additional ways you might polish your skills.

## Modelling – the study of excellence

Find a friend or colleague who is a master persuader. Study their behavioural patterns. How do they achieve their results? What is it that they are doing more of/less of that is different from people who are not as successful? What are the differences that make the difference?

Most areas of human excellence can be replicated. Once you have found a model:

- Watch and listen as your model persuades and influences. What are they doing (in terms of behaviour and physiology)? How are they doing it (in terms of language, internal thought processes, strategies)? What are their supporting beliefs and assumptions? Explore all these questions through observation and questions.

- Now remove elements of your model's behaviour. What is it that makes the difference? If you remove an aspect and it makes little or no difference, it is not important. If you take something out which will affect the result, then it is an essential part of the model's success.

- Test your findings, practise and polish them until they become a natural part of your influencing strategies and tactics.

## Sources for observation

Examples of Perfect Persuasion can be found all around us: in advertising, politics, debates and discussions, in literature, films, television, theatre. At meetings and in presentations. In letters, reports, proposals. All of these sources – and hundreds more – can provide you with excellent reference material for an indirect form of modelling.

- Films to watch: *Twelve Angry Men; Casablanca; The Shawshank Redemption; Dead Poets' Society; Field of Dreams; It's a Wonderful Life; Dangerous Liaisons*

- Plays to see: *Julius Caesar* (William Shakespeare); *Pygmalion* (George Bernard Shaw)

- Books to read:
  *Speeches That Changed the World* London: Quercus Publishing plc, 2005
  Kenney, A *Memories of a Militant* London: Edward Arnold, 1924 (out of print)*

* Books that are no longer in print can usually be sourced through www.abebooks.com or www.amazon.com

Bauby, J *The Diving Bell and The Butterfly* London: Fourth Estate, 1997

Ballard, J G *Empire of the Sun* London: Victor Gollancz, 1985

Kesey, K *One Flew Over the Cuckoo's Nest* London: Methuen & Co Ltd, 1962

Wollstonecraft, M *A Vindication of the Rights of Woman* London: Penguin, 2004

## Sources used in this book

Argyle, M *The Social Psychology of Everyday Life* London: Routledge, 1992

Aristotle; Lawson-Tancred, H (ed.) *The Art of Rhetoric* London: Penguin Classics, 1992

Bandler, R & La Valle, J *Persuasion Engineering* California: Meta Publications, 1996

Bradbury, A *Develop Your NLP Skills* London: Kogan Page, 2006

Buzan, T *The Mind Map Book* London: BBC Books, 1993

Carnegie, D *How to Win Friends and Influence People* London: Cedar Books, 1938

Charvet, S R *Words That Change Minds* USA: Kendall/Hunt Publishing, 1995

Cialdini, R B *Influence: Science and Practice* Massachusetts, USA: Allyn & Bacon, 2001

Heinrichs, J *Thank You for Arguing* London: Penguin, 2008

Knight, S *NLP at Work* London: Nicholas Brealey Publishing, 1996

Lakin, D *The Unfair Advantage* USA: Lakin Associates, 2000

O'Connor, J & Seymour, J *Introducing Neuro-Linguistic Programming,* London: Thorsons, 1995

O'Connor, J & Seymour, J *Training with NLP – skills for managers, trainers and communicators* London: Thorsons, 1994

Pease, A & B *The Definitive Book of Body Language* London: Orion Books, 2004

Richardson, J *The Magic of Rapport* California: Meta Publications, 1987

Storey, R *The Art of Persuasive Communication* London: Gower Publishing Ltd, 1997 (out of print)

Storey, R *Influencing Pocketbook* London: Management Pocketbooks Ltd., 2007

Thomson, L *Personality Type: An Owner's Manual* Boston: Shambala Publications, 1998

Wilder, C *The Presentations Kit: 10 Steps for Selling Your Ideas* New York: John Wiley & Sons, 1994

# Perfect Confidence

## Jan Ferguson

**All you need to get it right first time**

- Do you find it hard to stay calm under pressure?
- Are you worried that you don't always stand up for yourself?
- Do you want some straightforward advice on overcoming insecurities?

*Perfect Confidence* is the ideal companion for anyone who wants to boost their self-esteem. Covering everything from communicating clearly to handling conflict, it explains exactly why confidence matters and equips you with the skills you need to become more assertive. Whether you need to get ahead in the workplace or learn how to balance the demands of friends and family, *Perfect Confidence* has all you need to meet challenges head on.

The *Perfect* series is a range of practical guides that give clear and straightforward advice on everything from getting your first job to choosing your baby's name. Written by experienced authors offering tried-and-tested tips, each book contains all you need to get it right first time.

BOOKS

# Perfect Positive Thinking

## Lynn Williams

### All you need to know

- Are you troubled by negative thoughts?
- Do you find it hard to get motivated?
- Would you like some guidance on how to feel more upbeat?

*Perfect Positive Thinking* is essential reading for anyone who wants to feel optimistic and enthusiastic. Written by a professional life coach, with years of experience in the field, it gives practical advice on how to overcome negative feelings, explains how to deal with problems like anxiety and self-doubt, and provides helpful tips on how to gain energy, motivation and a sense of purpose. Covering everything from exercising to eating, and from stretching to sleep, *Perfect Positive Thinking* has all you need to feel happy and confident.

BOOKS

# Perfect Relaxation

## Elaine van der Zeil

**All you need to keep calm under pressure**

- Do you want to take control of your hectic lifestyle?
- Do you want to fight back against stress?
- Would you like some tips on how to be more relaxed?

*Perfect Relaxation* is an invaluable guide for anyone who wants to learn how to remain calm and powerful in challenging situations. Covering everything from how to stop obsessing to how to start thinking positively, it gives step-by-step guidance on beating stress and shows you how to make relaxation a part of your everyday life. With helpful suggestions for instant calming techniques and daily exercises to help combat tension, *Perfect Relaxation* has everything you need to bring your stress levels under control.

BOOKS